HIS STORY

Tracing the Scarlet Thread of God's Grace

HIS
STORY

Tracing the Scarlet Thread of God's Grace

Learner Guide

His Story: Tracing the Scarlet Thread of God's Grace (Learner Guide)
Copyright © 2024 by First Baptist Church Peachtree City in cooperation with Five Mark Ministries

Book Cover: Tonya Allen
Edited: Rachael Woodard
General Editor: Dr. Craig Hamlin

ISBN: 9798332151804
Imprint: Independently published

—

I am the Vine; you are the branches. If you abide in me and I in you, you will bear much fruit; apart from me, you can do nothing.
John 15:5

—

—

Table of Contents

—

Contributors

Lynn Burton
Noah and the Flood
Genesis 7:1-8:22

The Power of the Gospel
Romans 3:1-31; 5:1-21

Wayne Outlaw
The Covenant
Genesis 15:1-17:27

A Kinsman Redeemer
Ruth 1-4

Wendy Peters
The Crossing of the Red Sea
Exodus 13-14

Steve Rasmussen
The Idols of Our Worship
Exodus 32-33

Jesus is the One and Only
John 14:1-15:17

Madison Slay
The Great Kick Start
Acts 1:1-11; 2:1-47

Dr. Craig Hamlin
Imprisoned but Not Forgotten
Genesis 40-41

No Giant is Too Big
1 Samuel 17

The Lord is My Shepherd
Psalm 23

Who Do You Love?
Jonah 1-4

How to Use This Learner's Guide

The Learner Guide for *His Story* is designed to maximize your study of the *His Story* curriculum. There are specific elements for you to engage interactively on a personal level, as well as, with your small group. This Learner's Guide is set up with some featured components:

Connecting to the Story – this helps you with some introductory questions to get you thinking about the story and its application.

Diving into the Story – this helps you learn what the story is about with the outline and Scripture passages.

Diving Deeper – these are questions to give you a major takeaway and practical next steps as you think through what you have learned.

Use the space provided with questions to write down your thoughts. At the end of each chapter, there are **GROW** Scriptures. These Scriptures correspond to the **GROW** workbooks on which *His Story* is based. An additional resource is the **GROW** books that are designed to be used with a smaller group of men and women in an organic bible-study, life-to-life setting.

For more information on how to purchase **GROW** materials, visit **www.joeyrodgers.com**.

Introduction to His Story

The story of the Bible is without a doubt the greatest of all love stories. For in the pages of Scripture, we discover that God so loved each and every one of us so much that He willingly humbled Himself by stepping out of heaven and into flesh to do what only He could do to reconcile His creation back to Himself through a sovereign act of grace. So, whether we realize it or not, when we pick up God's Word, we are being given a front-row seat to the scarlet thread of God's redemptive plan for all of humanity. From the very first verse in Genesis 1, to the last verse in Revelation, we are privy to the spectacular narrative of God's relentless pursuit of His creation. In His-Story, we discover who He is, who we are, how we have fallen, and the means by which God makes a satisfactory atonement by grace through faith. Likewise, we discover the difference between good and evil, right and wrong, and what is of God and what is not of God.

Oftentimes though, there is a misnomer that the Bible is a book of history – yet this would not be accurate. While the Bible is historically true and archeologically sound, it is not a full rendering of history. Likewise, while it is scientifically accurate, it is not a book of science. Instead, the Bible is nothing less than a recounting of God's story of mercy and grace. It is the story of how God has progressively moved through time to redeem that which was lost in the fall. Of course, throughout the Bible, we see God intersecting and interacting with mankind in amazing and miraculous ways to reveal Himself and His will and plan in general and personally for each of us. So, this story matters… His story matters because eternity literally hangs in the balance.

Over the next 12 weeks, I want to invite you to walk through the narrative of the Bible to begin to understand its truths and relevance to your life. Certainly, many of these stories are going to be familiar. Thus, my hope is that over this time, God will rekindle your heart and afford you an appreciation of His relentless pursuit of your heart and affection. As you revisit these stories and persons you may have learned as a child, it is my prayer that God will move to mature your understanding by giving you a new insight into your faith today. I look forward to the journey as we see the big picture of God's grace and as we plunge into the depths of His immensity.

Blessings,
Dr. Joey Rodgers

SESSION 1

Noah and the Flood

Genesis 7:1-8:22

J.R.R. Tolkien, the author of *The Lord of the Rings* trilogy once wrote, "The greatest adventure is what lies ahead." Tolkien lived this adventure through his fantasy world of hobbits, wizards and middle Earth. He sent the reader on an adventure of epic proportion from one land and one kingdom after another, all in an effort to bring peace to the world and protection from the personification of man's evil heart. Tolkien's main character, Frodo Baggins, a cautious but respectful Hobbit, became a symbol of hope, someone who would not give in to the lure of the ring of power. Frodo carried the ring around his neck like an anchor weighing down every step until he could vanquish it forever in the fires of Mordor. In *The Fellowship of the Ring*, Galadriel says of Frodo, "Even the smallest person can change the course of the future."

Such are the stories of triumph like that of Gideon and his army of 300 against the million-man force of the Midianites, and of David, who as a ruddy young shepherd faces a nine feet tall giant named Goliath. And such is Noah, who among all the people in a world gone mad with gluttonous self-indulgence and violence, listens to the voice of God and builds a boat in the desert.

Noah's story is one of obedience, fulfilled promise, worship and salvation. Throughout Noah's adventure with God, he must fight against his detractors and critics to trust God in what must seem to be a risky venture. And yet, Noah finds favor in the eyes of the Lord because he knows his life and his family's life can only be saved through the refuge of God's will. His Story will take you through the greatest adventure of all that is God's redemptive story. The ark will symbolize the cross and the crashing waves flooding the earth, God's judgment. All who are in the ark are safe but those outside the ark will be lost. When God poured out His wrath on Jesus dying on the cross, Jesus opened His arms of forgiveness so that all those who come to Him by faith might be saved. From Noah's story until the cross of Jesus, God has woven this scarlet thread through history, people, prophets and prophecies. Has His thread been woven into your heart and your story?

 Connecting to the Story

How is it possible to live like Noah in a wicked and godless culture? How are ways you can impact your culture for transformation?

Diving into the Story

What's It All About

"*In the beginning*" captures the very definition of the Book of Genesis, which means the origin or coming into being of something. In this case, the very beginning of existence, of earth, creation and mankind. The first chapter captures the heart of a creative God who repeatably says of His creation, "It is good."

However, creation as God intended was quickly broken when sin entered into the Garden. Adam and Eve at this point disobeyed God's command and broke the intimacy of relationship with Him. "Then the man and his wife heard the sound of the LORD God as he was walking in the garden in the cool of the day, and they hid from the LORD God among the trees of the garden. But the LORD God called to the man, "Where are you" (Gen. 3:9)?

The Book of Genesis is an appropriate introduction to the entire Bible. Answers can be found in its 50 chapters about the origins of the universe, ourselves, all life forms, sin and the evils in the world. Though not intended as a scientific document, Genesis is very clear that all things were created and had a definite beginning point—God. Kent Dobson wrote, "The creation narratives teach that life is a gift from God, with whom we are in relationship. The experience of Adam and Eve mirrors the discovery of our own moral responsibility, our loss of innocence, the pains of rearing children, the necessity of working with our own hands and the knowledge of our own mortality. We discover in the story that we have all eaten from the tree, and we all hide from God."

God's question of "where are you" would be asked again of Cain in chapter 4. The creeping tentacles of sin now spread to the next generation. It would be this spreading that would infect the next generations until we reach the generation of Noah. Finally, the heartbreaking words, "The LORD saw how great the wickedness of the human race had become on the earth, and that every inclination of the thoughts of the human heart was only evil all the time. The LORD regretted that he had made human beings on the earth, and his heart was deeply troubled. So, the LORD said, "I will wipe from the face of the earth the human race I have created—and with them the animals, the birds and the creatures that moved along the ground—for I regret that I have made them." (Gen 6:5-8)

There had been few bright spots in the generations and notably, Enoch was one of those bright spots. Among the genealogy of chapter 5 it was recorded that "Enoch walked faithfully with God 300 years and had other sons and daughters." (Gen 5:22) The key to his relationship with God was summed up in verse 24, "Enoch walked faithfully with God; then he was no more, because God took him away." The total depravity of humankind would bring God to the ultimate decision that all of life would be destroyed. Yet it would be Enoch's great grandson Noah that would become a beacon of hope for mankind. As God speaks the words, "for I regret that I have made them," they are followed by the simple phrase, "But Noah found favor in the eyes of the LORD." (6:8)

Scripture records that "Noah was a righteous man, blameless among the people of his time, and he walked faithfully with God"(6:9). Little was known of his occupation, background or personal preferences. We do know he was married and had three sons, Shem, Ham and Japheth. However, what we do know was critical and the most important qualities of who Noah was as a man. Scripture described him as righteous, blameless and faithful. Characteristics that would not be easy in light of the culture in which he lived at the time. The culture that Noah lived in was described as corrupt in God's sight and full of violence.

The Big Idea

Living in a culture that was defined as wicked and every intent of the citizens was evil, Noah made the conscious decision to seek God with all his heart, soul and mind. In so doing, Noah found favor with God and became a source of salvation for his family.

Christ in the Text

Jesus Christ became the ark of our salvation through his dying on the cross. Just as God closed the door on the ark to save Noah and his family, Jesus closed the door of death for those who enter his salvation. "I am the way, and the truth, and the life; no one comes to the Father, but through Me." (John 14:6)

#1 Obedience

"By faith Noah, being warned by God concerning events as yet unseen, in reverent fear constructed an ark for the saving of his household. By this he condemned the world and became an heir of the righteousness that comes by faith."
~ Genesis 11:7

1. At what point does obedience begin?

2. When God told Noah to enter the ark, he faced societal pressure that pressed against his faith. What are some ways Christians face societal pressure that presses against their faith?

3. How do you survive and thrive with obedient faith in a culture bent on pursuing self-interest and godlessness? What does the Christlike love look like in this culture?

2 Salvation

"So make yourself an ark of cypress wood; make rooms in it and coat it with pitch inside and out.... I am going to bring floodwaters on the earth to destroy all life under the heavens, every creature that has the breath of life in it. Everything on earth will perish."
~ Gen 6:14-17

"Then the LORD shut him in."
~ Genesis 7:16b

1. How does the ark symbolize salvation for both humanity and creation?

2. At what point did Noah experience salvation?

3. How does obedience to God play a role in salvation when salvation is by grace through faith alone apart from works?

#3 Promise

"The LORD smelled the pleasing aroma and said in his heart: "Never again will I curse the ground because of humans, even though every inclination of the human heart is evil from childhood. And never again will I destroy all living creatures, as I have done. As long as the earth endures, seedtime and harvest, cold and heat, summer and winter, day and night will never cease." ~ **Gen 8:21-22**

1. What does God's promise say about his character?

2. Knowing the promise of God to not destroy the world again through a flood, what are ways humanity continues in their self-destructive way toward the planet and toward humanity?

3. Read Isaiah 54:7-10. How did God live up to His promise? How are you living up to your promise to God?

#4 Worship

"Then God said to Noah, 'Go out from the ark, you and your wife, and your sons and your sons' wives with you. Bring out with you every living thing that is with you of all flesh — birds and animals and every creeping thing that creeps on the earth — that they may swarm on the earth.' So Noah went out, and his sons and his wife and his sons' wives with him. Every beast, every creeping thing, and every bird, everything that moves on the earth, went out by families from the ark. Then Noah built an altar to the Lord and took some of every clean animal and some of every clean bird and offered burnt offerings on the altar. And when the Lord smelled the pleasing aroma, the Lord said in his heart, 'I will never again curse the ground because of man, for the intention of man's heart is evil from his youth. Neither will I ever again strike down every living creature as I have done. While the earth remains, seedtime and harvest, cold and heat, summer and winter, day and night, shall not cease.'"

~ *Genesis 8:15-22*

1. Where do you place worship as a priority in your daily life?

2. How does worship make a difference in your attitude, outlook and actions?

⑨ Diving Deeper

1. What is the biggest takeaway from this passage?

2. What are some ways you could apply this passage?

3. In what ways does Noah's story inspire or challenge you in your walk with God?

4. What will you apply specifically this week?

5. Who will hold you accountable this week for your response to Question 4?

"Unless we are thoroughly convinced that without Christ we are under the eternal curse of God, as the worst of His enemies, we shall never flee to Him for refuge."
~ John Owen

🦶 GROW Passages for Week 1

1. Genesis 1:1-31

2. Genesis 2:1-25

3. Genesis 3:1-4:26

4. Genesis 7:1-8:22

5. Genesis 11:1-9

SESSION 2

The Covenant

Genesis 15:1-17:27

Every person who has walked down the aisle or stood before someone vowing to keep their love sacred before God as long as they live have entered into a covenant with God. While some only see marriage through the lens of a contract, the Lord takes marriage much more seriously. Why? God is a covenant-making God! Professor Bruce Shelley makes the distinction between contracts and covenants in biblical terms. He writes, "In modern times we define a host of relations by contracts. These are usually for goods or services and for hard cash. The contract, formal or informal, helps to specify failure in these relationships. The Lord did not establish a contract with Israel or with the church. He created a covenant.

There is a difference. Contracts are broken when one of the parties fails to keep his promise. If, let us say, a patient fails to keep an appointment with a doctor, the doctor is not obligated to call the house and inquire, "Where were you? Why didn't you show up for your appointment?" He simply goes on to his next patient and has his appointment secretary take note of the patient who failed to keep the appointment. The patient may find it harder the next time to see the doctor. He broke an informal contract.

According to the Bible, however, the Lord asks: "Can a mother forget the baby at her breast and have no compassion on the child she has borne? Though she may forget, I will not forget you!" (Isaiah 49:15)

The Bible indicates the covenant is more like the ties of a parent to her child than it is a doctor's appointment. If a child fails to show up for dinner, the parent's obligation, unlike the doctor's, isn't canceled. The parent finds out where the child is and makes sure he's cared for. One member's failure does not destroy the relationship. A covenant puts no conditions on faithfulness. It is the unconditional commitment to love and serve."

In the next installment of His Story's metanarrative, God shows Himself as a covenant-making God. His ultimate expression of covenant promise reveals itself in God's sacrificial death on the cross, fulfilling His promise to redeem humanity once and for all (Genesis 3). In this story, you see God making His promise to Abraham and then symbolizing it through circumcision. In this act, God foreshadows the blood He will shed on our behalf to secure our redemption and fulfill His promise to us as our Faithful Redeemer!

Connecting to the Story

What has been a promise made to you that was broken? Why is fulfilling your promises so critical to life and to knowing the character of God?

Diving into the Story

What's It All About

Abram received an astonishing revelation from God. He tells Abram to leave his own country, relatives, and his father's house and enter a strange land that God will reveal. And God declares that He will bring Abram to glory, with a great name, a great nation of people, a man of strength; moreover, through Abram, all the families and nations of the earth will be blessed. That was the first of seven times God would meet with Abram (later Abraham).

God tells Abram that he must first begin this chain of events by taking a step of obedience and leaving his country of Ur. God's plan to use Abram depends on him leaving everything in the world in which Abram finds his identity and security. He must obey God's voice, depend on God's promises, and rely on His provision. Abram took that step of faith.

As he moves around in the land, Abram is tested by many crises, and God grows him as a man of faith. We also see Abram's growth in the light of God's grace! Abraham is now ready to receive a covenant from God. God appears to Abraham for the fourth time, and the occasion for the visitation is similar to the previous three visits: God's Covenant with Abram. But with this visit, God is ready to bring Abram the full revelation of His covenant, including a sign that Abram will carry in his body to show that God has made this promise to him and his family.

The Big Idea

God formalizes His promise to Abraham with an official commitment called a covenant. God invites Abraham to look up at the night stars and count them, saying that's how numerous his family will become. Up until this point in time, Abraham has no children, and he and his wife, Sarah, have no way to produce children.

Despite these very bad odds, Abraham looks up and simply trusts God's promise. God graciously responds by entering into a covenant with him, promising that Abraham will become a father of many nations and that God's blessing may come to the whole world. He asks Abraham to mark his family with the "sign of the covenant," or the circumcision of all males, as a symbol to remind them that their fruitfulness comes from God.

Christ in the Text

Since the fall in the Garden in Genesis, God made the promise to bring a Messiah to rectify the sin of Adam. That promise progressed from one son to another and so on. Finally, it landed on Abraham. And here the promise takes form. There would be a people, set in a land, which would bring forth the blessing of the promise on behalf of the entire world.

All nations would be blessed through the descendants of Abraham. After Jacob, the promise would be extended to 12 sons. While the promise of the Messiah is carried forward through only the line of Judah, the promises for blessing and the land are extended to many descendants. Through the line of Judah, Jesus Christ, rectified the sin of Adam.

#1 The Blessings of the Covenant (17:1-8)

When Abram was ninety-nine years old the LORD appeared to Abram and said to him, "I am God Almighty; walk before me, and be blameless, that I may make my covenant between me and you, and may multiply you greatly." Then Abram fell on his face. And God said to him, "Behold, my covenant is with you, and you shall be the father of a multitude of nations. No longer shall your name be called Abram, but your name shall be Abraham, for I have made you the father of a multitude of nations. I will make you exceedingly fruitful, and I will make you into nations, and kings shall come from you. And I will establish my covenant between me and you and your offspring after you throughout their generations for an everlasting covenant, to be God to you and to your offspring after you. And I will give to you and to your offspring after you the land of your sojournings, all the land of Canaan, for an everlasting possession, and I will be their God."
~ Genesis 17:1-8

1. What does God's choice of Abraham tell us about His sovereign plans?

2. Why do you think God chose to change Abram's name to Abraham?

2 The Rite of Circumcision (17:9-14)

And God said to Abraham, "As for you, you shall keep my covenant, you and your offspring after you throughout their generations. This is my covenant, which you shall keep, between me and you and your offspring after you: Every male among you shall be circumcised. You shall be circumcised in the flesh of your foreskins, and it shall be a sign of the covenant between me and you. He who is eight days old among you shall be circumcised. Every male throughout your generations, whether born in your house or bought with your money from any foreigner who is not of your offspring, both he who is born in your house and he who is bought with your money, shall surely be circumcised. So shall my covenant be in your flesh an everlasting covenant. Any uncircumcised male who is not circumcised in the flesh of his foreskin shall be cut off from his people; he has broken my covenant."
~ Genesis 17:9-14

1. What is the significance of circumcision as the sign of the covenant?

2. What does it represent?

#3 The Promise of an Heir (17:15-21)

And God said to Abraham, "As for Sarai your wife, you shall not call her name Sarai, but Sarah shall be her name. I will bless her, and moreover, I will give you a son by her. I will bless her, and she shall become nations; kings of peoples shall come from her." Then Abraham fell on his face and laughed and said to himself, "Shall a child be born to a man who is a hundred years old?

Shall Sarah, who is ninety years old, bear a child?" And Abraham said to God, "Oh that Ishmael might live before you!" God said, "No, but Sarah your wife shall bear you a son, and you shall call his name Isaac. I will establish my covenant with him as an everlasting covenant for his offspring after him. As for Ishmael, I have heard you; behold, I have blessed him and will make him fruitful and multiply him greatly. He shall father twelve princes, and I will make him into a great nation. But I will establish my covenant with Isaac, whom Sarah shall bear to you at this time next year."
~ Genesis 17:15-21

1. How do Abraham's reaction of laughter and doubt reflect human responses to God's supernatural promises?

2. How did God show both firmness and compassion to Abraham's request to use Ishmael as the covenant son?

#4 Abraham's Affirmation of the Covenant (17:22-27)

When he had finished talking with him, God went up from Abraham. Then Abraham took Ishmael his son and all those born in his house or bought with his money, every male among the men of Abraham's house, and he circumcised the flesh of their foreskins that very day, as God had said to him. Abraham was ninety-nine years old when he was circumcised in the flesh of his foreskin. And Ishmael his son was thirteen years old when he was circumcised in the flesh of his foreskin. That very day Abraham and his son Ishmael were circumcised. And all the men of his house, those born in the house and those bought with money from a foreigner, were circumcised with him.
~ Genesis 17:22-27

1. How does Abraham's immediate obedience inspire you in your faith journey?

2. What are the ways we can affirm our faith in Christ in a society which seeks autonomy from God?

⑨ Diving Deeper

1. What is the biggest takeaway from this passage?

2. What are some ways you could apply this passage?

3. In what ways does Abraham's story inspire or challenge you in your walk with God?

4. What will you apply specifically this week?

5. Who will hold you accountable this week for your response to Question 4?

"Simply stated, the covenant of redemption is a covenant God the Father made with God the Son before the foundation of the world was laid, that is, the Son would offer Himself as an offering for sin, and the Father would give Christ all those for whom He would die as a gift of love."
~ Don Kistler

⑨ GROW Passages for Week 2

1. Genesis 11:27-12:20

2. Genesis 13:1-14:24

3. Genesis 15:1-17:27

4. Genesis 18:1-19:29

5. Genesis 21:1-21; 22:1-19

SESSION 3

Imprisoned but Not Forgotten

Genesis 40:1-41:57

Admiral Jim Stockdale, the highest-ranking officer in the Hanoi Hilton prisoner of war camp during the pinnacle of the Vietnam War, was interviewed by Jim Collins, the author of *Good to Great*. When Collins asked Admiral Stockdale about life in the war camp, Collins asked, "Who didn't make it out?" Stockdale quickly answered, "Oh, that's easy. The optimists." Puzzled, Collins asked the Admiral to elaborate. "The optimists. Oh, they were the ones who said, 'We're going to be out by Christmas.' And Christmas would come, and Christmas would go. Then they'd say, 'We're going to be out by Easter.' And Easter would come, and Easter would go. And then Thanksgiving, and then it would be Christmas again. And they died of a broken heart. This is a very important lesson. You must never confuse faith that you will prevail in the end—which you can never afford to lose—with the discipline to confront the most brutal facts of your current reality, whatever they might be." Joseph's life was one of adversity starting with his dysfunctional family to the unfair treatment he received for years in prison under a false charge and forgetful prison mate. And yet, not one time did Joseph succumb to the pressure of false optimism. He lived in the reality that the Lord was with him. Joseph did not desire the pain, but knew that the struggle would produce a better outcome.

When you walk through adversity, the last thing you should do is try to avoid the struggle. In the struggle, you can rejoice, "knowing that suffering produces endurance, and endurance produces character, and character

20

produces hope" (Romans 5:3-4). Christians in the West often miss this point, because we live in the most medicated country in the world. While pain is never welcomed and adversity is never sought after, they cause us to grow stronger. Joseph walked a hard path, but every step of the way, he was growing and God was using him to make a major impact. What could God be bringing you through where he reminds you that you are not alone, but also, you are being fashioned into a sharper tool ready to be used for God's purposes? Allow God to bring you into and through the ups and downs of life without complaining and with the anticipation of learning from the Master.

Connecting to the Story

What's the difference between someone who always likes to play the victim and someone who has truly been victimized?

Diving into the Story

What's It All About
The story of Joseph is the longest narrative in Genesis. It covers well over almost 100 years from the time Joseph was a young man living in Mesopotamia and hated by his brothers to him living in Egypt until he was 110 years old with three generations surrounding him at his death. The story of Joseph's imprisonment is one moment in a sea of moments that shined the spotlight on God's sovereign plan for his people, and moments foreshadowing the life and ministry of the coming Messiah.

Joseph is a type of Messiah or type of Christ. Both were prophesied to be rulers (Gen. 37:5-11; Daniel 7:13-14; Micah 4:7; 5:2). Their brothers were jealous and did not believe them (Gen. 37:4-5, 11; John 7:3-5). Both were targets of persecution and attempts on their life (Genesis 37; Acts 2:22-23). Joseph was sold into slavery in Egypt. Jesus was betrayed for the price of a slave (Gen. 37:26-28; Matthew 26:15). Both were falsely accused (Gen.

39:11-20; Matthew 26:59-61). Both suffered with two others (Gen. 40:1-3, 20-22; Luke 23:32, 39-43). Joseph and Jesus declared the path to life (Gen. 41:33; John 5:54; 6:35). The Spirit of God dwelled in them both (Gen. 41:38; Luke 4:1). All knees bowed to Joseph. All knees will bow to Jesus (Gen. 41:43; Phil. 2:10). Both offered forgiveness to those who sought to destroy them (Gen. 45:5-8; 50:20; Luke 23:34; Acts 5:31).

Many other signs and typologies appear in the study of Joseph's life that mirrors Jesus. Jesus, however, supersedes Joseph as the God-man who lived a perfect life and died a substitutionary, atoning death for all mankind, culminating in a victorious bodily resurrection. Therefore, knowing that Joseph is a fore-shadowing figure in the Old Testament, the story of Joseph's life is magnified as a story that points to the ultimate Savior of all mankind. But in the Genesis account, readers are able to see the impact of one man's life fully surrendered to God and the character that results from one who came from troubled beginnings to be the deliverer of his people from certain death.

Joseph was the son of Jacob, the son of Isaac who was the son of Abraham. Jacob had several wives through whom he eventually had twelve sons. Joseph was the son of Jacob and Rachel (Gen. 35:24). Joseph had one "blood" brother, Benjamin who was also born to Jacob and Rachel. In Genesis 37, Joseph is introduced at the age of 17. He was a shepherd with his brothers, loved by his father more than all the others (Gen. 37:3) and told his brothers that they would one day bow to him (Gen. 37:5-11). Joseph's brothers hated him for his perceived arrogance and sought to kill him. However, they faked his death, sold him into slavery and convinced his father that Joseph had been eaten by a wild animal. Joseph was sold to merchants headed to Egypt.

Eventually, Joseph was sold into Potiphar's house, the captain of Pharoah's guard. Throughout Joseph's enslavement, Scripture tells us, "The Lord was with Joseph" (Gen. 39:3, 21, 23). Even when Joseph is falsely accused of rape by Potiphar's wife, the Lord continued to watch over Joseph as he languished in prison for well over two years. As a result of the Lord's work in Joseph's life, the lessons of redemption and grace show the reader that Joseph might have been imprisoned, but he was not forgotten. In prison, Joseph demonstrated godly care for others, experienced heartbreak that could not break him and exhibited fruitfulness that led a nation and surrounding nations to survive massive famine. In the midst of it all, the Lord uses Joseph to deliver his family and set the next generations toward another major moment in God's redemptive plan 400 years later.

What can you learn during difficult moments of life, when nothing seems to be going right and injustice prevails on every side? When the Lord is with you and life is fruitful, things do not seem so desperate and your reliance on the Lord seemingly unnecessary. However, the disciple of Jesus knows that in every season of life there is the need for dependency on the Lord who walks with you through the hardships of life and provides guidance to develop endurance, character and grace through you.

The Big Idea
Life is hard, but when we walk with God through dark times, we know He never abandons us but uses the suffering to develop a greater endurance for more significant ministry moments.

Christ in the Text
Jesus suffered monumental hardships at the hands of those who rejected Him, but in His compassion and grace, Jesus patiently delivered those who rejected Him from the prison of their sin and the famine of their soul.

#1 When the Lord is with You, You Develop Character to Care for Others Even When No One Cares for You (40:1-8)

"Sometime after this, the cupbearer of the king of Egypt and his baker committed an offense against their lord the king of Egypt. And Pharaoh was angry with his two officers, the chief cupbearer and the chief baker, and he put them in custody in the house of the captain of the guard, in the prison where Joseph was confined.

The captain of the guard appointed Joseph to be with them, and he attended them. They continued for some time in custody. And one night they both dreamed—the cupbearer and the baker of the king of Egypt, who were confined in the prison—each his own dream, and each dream with its own interpretation. When Joseph came to them in the morning, he saw that they were troubled.

So he asked Pharaoh's officers who were with him in custody in his master's house, "Why are your faces downcast today?" They said to him, "We have had dreams, and there is no one to interpret them." And Joseph said to them, "Do not interpretations belong to God? Please tell them to me."
~ Genesis 40:1-8

1. What is your natural response to tough situations in life?

2. Do you tend to isolate or get angry in tough situations?

3. How do you move past your raw emotions to seek God's development of your character during trials you face?

2 When the Lord is with You, You Rise Above Personal Disappointments and Heartbreaks to Moments of Significant Ministry (40:9-41:36)

"They said to him, 'We have had dreams, and there is no one to interpret them.' And Joseph said to them, 'Do not interpretations belong to God? Please tell them to me'...Yet the chief cupbearer did not remember Joseph but forgot him."
~ Genesis 40:8, 23

1. Why is it so hard to wait on the Lord when it seems no relief is in sight?

2. What have you learned in those moments of waiting that God used for His glory, your good, and the good of others?

#3 When the Lord is with You, You Experience and Exhibit Fruitfulness through the Work of the Holy Spirit (41:37-57)

"Joseph called the name of the firstborn Manasseh. 'For', he said, 'God has made me forget all my hardship and all my father's house.' The name of the second he called Ephraim, 'For God has made me fruitful in the land of my affliction'."
~ Genesis 41:51-52

1. How have you seen the Holy Spirit at work in your life through the hardships you have faced?

2. What lessons did you learn that could be helpful to others?

3. Why is it important for others to see the Holy Spirit at work in you?

Diving Deeper

1. What is the biggest takeaway from this passage?

2. What are some ways you could apply this passage?

3. How does the knowledge that "the Lord is with you" influence the way you live everyday?

4. What will you apply specifically this week?

5. Who will hold you accountable this week for your response to Question 4?

God never calls you to a task without giving you what you need to do it.
He never sends you without going with you.
~ Paul David Tripp

GROW Passages for Week 3

1. Genesis 25:19-34; 26:34-28:9

2. Genesis 32:22-32

3. Genesis 37:1-36

4. Genesis 39:1-23

5. Genesis 40:1-41:57

SESSION 4

The Crossing of the Red Sea

Exodus 13:1-14:31

In his book, *Six Hours One Friday*, Max Lucado tells the story of a missionary in Brazil who ministered to a remote tribe of Indians. The village was experiencing a deadly and contagious disease that threatened to eradicate the entire population. The missionary knew the cure was close but the natives would have to follow him across a river that they believed to be cursed. The missionary told them that he had crossed it many times, but they would not believe. Finally, the missionary jumped in the river, submerged himself and swam to the other side. When the natives saw this, they leapt into the water and followed the missionary to find the cure.

There are times when you face insurmountable obstacles and challenges. Fear, doubt, and anxiety fill your mind and paralyze your faith. What people fail to realize is the power of God and His willingness to step into your impossible situations because He loves you. People love to believe they can handle their problems on their own. They believe they are the only ones who know best how to solve the crisis, but then you come across a situation that is impossible.

Do you fall apart or fall into the arms of God? The crossing of the Red Sea was one of those moments when God demonstrated His power, love and grace to His people. The event pictured the rescue of God, not by their own strength, but by the awesome power of Almighty God.

The crossing pictured what Jesus did when He did what only He could do, die as the perfect sacrifice, and be raised from the dead on our behalf. Jesus submerged himself in the river of your sinfulness to prove His love for you. As Lucado writes, "Jesus saw people enslaved by their fear of death. He explained that death was nothing to fear. He called Lazarus out of the grave yet they were still cynical. He had to submerge himself in the water of death before people would believe that death had been conquered. And he came out on the other side of death's river. He proved once and for all, our death, is not final."

 # Connecting to the Story

What is the greatest need that people face in their day to day lives? What is a seemingly insurmountable obstacle you have faced in your life, and what was the outcome?

 # Diving into the Story

What's It All About
As God prepared the Israelite nation for another awesome display of His power in the parting of the Red Sea, He also wanted them to undeniably know and remember that He was their great Redeemer. Therefore, in scripture, the Lord instituted the ceremonies of Israel's deliverance: the Passover (12:1-13), the Feast of the Unleavened Bread (12:14-20 & 13:3-10) and the Consecration of the Firstborn (13:1-2, 11-16). It is imperative to highlight these ceremonies to gain a fuller understanding of the Exodus story.

Passover
God promised to redeem His people from the bondage of Egyptian slavery (Genesis15:13-14 & Exodus 6:6). When Pharaoh refused freedom to the Israelites, God sent the ten plagues to reveal His power, authority, and sovereignty.

The Passover ceremony was directed by God for the Israelite people to perform in preparation for the tenth and final plague that God would bring upon Egypt the night before the Exodus. The Israelites were to select a perfect male, one-year-old sheep or goat to be killed and its blood be applied to the doorposts and lintels (horizontal beam) of the houses.

Then when the Lord passed throughout Egypt, He would literally, "pass over the door and would not allow the destroyer to come" (12:23) into households that had the blood covering. In order for Israel to be spared the judgment of the firstborn they had to believe and do what God prescribed in the Passover sacrifice. The Israelites were commanded to always observe this event with their families (12:24) and when asked why they were required to perform this ceremony by their children they were to reply, "It is the Passover offering to the LORD through which we were redeemed." The Passover ceremony, celebrated in the first month of the Hebrew calendar, was a chance for God to be remembered as the great Deliverer and Redeemer.

Feast of the Unleavened Bread

The inception of this ceremony occurs in Exodus 12, although the instructions for this memorial feast are found in Leviticus 23:6-8, Numbers 28:16-25, and Deuteronomy 16:1-8. This ceremony, like Passover, was to serve as a reminder of God's power and provision as shown in the Exodus. Passover was to be celebrated at sunset on the 14th day of Nisan (formerly known as Abib) and was to be followed immediately by the Feast of Unleavened Bread, which would last for an additional seven days.

During this time no leaven (yeast) was to be eaten or even found within the households of the Israelites. (12:15,19 & 13:7) Unleavened bread could be made very quickly as the yeast would not need time to ferment and rise. Since the Jews had to be ready to make a hasty departure from Egypt, unleavened bread fit the bill.

In Deuteronomy 16:3 we see the reason why the Israelites were commanded to eat unleavened bread, *"Do not eat it with bread made with yeast, but for seven days eat unleavened bread, the bread of affliction, because you left Egypt in haste—so that all the days of your life you may remember the time of your departure from Egypt."*

John MacArthur also notes that the unleavened bread has a spiritual connotation. "Leaven in the Bible is always seen as influence, permeating influence, such as how leaven permeates dough, and usually it's bad. Unleavened bread, then, is a symbol of leaving behind all the permeating evil influence of Egypt." This unleavened bread then symbolized purity and sinlessness and points us to another sinless bread. In the Gospel of John, "Jesus declares Himself as the "bread of life." (John 6:35) Jesus, the perfect unleavened bread, lived a sinless life so that He in unexplainable grace could offer Himself as a willing sacrifice for our sin. Therefore, just as the Israelites were called to remove every trace of leaven from their houses during the Feast of Unleavened Bread, we too should remove sin from our lives and live a life of holiness and sanctification.

Consecration of the Firstborn

This ceremony, as with the two preceding ones, was to commemorate the death of the firstborn in Egypt, and the Lord's deliverance of Israel. Firstborn sons were very important in ancient times as they signified the future of the family. The oldest son had special responsibilities and privileges including the right of inheritance. Therefore, knowing the great value placed on the firstborn, the question then becomes, "Why does God just claim ownership over the firstborn?" As Philip Ryken describes, "The point of consecrating the firstborn was really to show that the whole family belonged to God. The firstborn stood for the family as a part representing the whole - the way, for example, that a captain represents his team at the beginning of a football game, or an executive represents his corporation at the bargaining table." Thus, when God commanded the consecration of the firstborn both of "man and beast" (13:1), the Lord was really proclaiming His ownership over the entirety of the nation of Israel.

This idea of the firstborn being the representative of the family also applies to the Egyptians. With the death of the firstborn, God pronounced judgement on the nation of Egypt. B.C. Newton notes that, "By striking dead each family's representative, Yahweh was placing each family under the sentence of death, which means that they were not being dramatic back in 12:23 when they said, "We shall all be dead." It turns out that they very clearly understood the message that God had sent."

With each consecration of the firstborn the Jews were remembering not only that God had delivered them from death, but also that they were called to be set apart; to be holy. Throughout scripture people and things are called holy because of their relationship to God. Israel was a holy nation only because they belonged to God. Thus, consecrating their firstborn generation after generation was a reminder and a "visible declaration of that spiritual reality."

The Red Sea
Having understood the significance of the three ceremonies of remembrance, it is also important to focus on the undeniable miracle of the parting of the Red Sea. In order to gain greater knowledge of this event and understand the Old Testament significance that points to New Testament truths, the account will be divided into three major sections:

#1   God's sovereign deliverance in times of seemingly impossible situations

#2   The Red Sea as a symbol of salvation

#3   Walking by faith through the parted waters

Before the study of these three divisions, it is essential to note that the historical works from the Old Testament in the Bible are not only intended to teach God's people the infallible truth of what happened historically, but also to foreshadow what happens spiritually as God deals with His people and the world at large.

This Exodus account is not just a record of history, but also a glorious illustration of things God does in the Christian heart. As C.H. Spurgeon expounds, "We look upon the book of Exodus as being a book of types of the deliverances which God will give to His elect people: not only as a history of what He has done in bringing them out of Egypt by smiting the firstborn, leading them through the Red Sea, and guiding them through the wilderness, but also as a picture of His faithful dealings with all His people, whom by the blood of Christ He separates from the Egyptians, and by His strong and mighty hand takes out of the house of their bondage and out of the land of their slavery."

The Big Idea

God's supreme power on display in the Exodus account shows His faithfulness and love in this story of redemption of God's chosen nation (Deut. 7:7-8). Just as Israel had to depend on God for provision and freedom from slavery, we too must look to God to provide freedom from the power of sin.

Christ in the Text

Jesus Christ is the ultimate Redeemer. Jesus Christ is the one and only way to spiritual salvation. (John 14:6)

#1 God's Sovereign Deliverance in Times of Seemingly Impossible Situations (13:1-14:4)

Then the LORD said to Moses, "Tell the people of Israel to turn back and encamp in front of Pi-hahiroth, between Migdol and the sea, in front of Baal-zephon; you shall encamp facing it, by the sea. For Pharaoh will say of the people of Israel, 'They are wandering in the land; the wilderness has shut them in.' And I will harden Pharaoh's heart, and he will pursue them, and I will get glory over Pharaoh and all his host, and the Egyptians shall know that I am the LORD." And they did so.

~ Exodus 14:1-4

1. Why does God, in His sovereignty, often bring us to hard places of trial, desperation and need?

2. In what ways does God's providence supply confidence when faced with impossible situations?

2 The Red Sea as a Symbol of Salvation (14:13-21)

"And Moses said to the people, 'Fear not, stand firm, and see the salvation of the Lord, which he will work for you today. For the Egyptians whom you see today, you shall never see again. The Lord will fight for you, and you have only to be silent.' The Lord said to Moses, 'Why do you cry to me? Tell the people of Israel to go forward. Lift up your staff, and stretch out your hand over the sea and divide it, that the people of Israel may go through the sea on dry ground."
~ Exodus 14:13-16

1. What is it about the salvation of the Lord that allows you to stand firm without fear?

2. Was the 'rod of God' in Moses hands the salvation of Israel? In other words, did their salvation come from Moses' power to wield the rod? Why do we live as if our salvation is up to us or the power for living the Christian life is up to us? What is the reality?

#3 Walking by Faith Through the Parted Waters (14:22-31)

"Thus, the Lord saved Israel that day, from the hand of the Egyptians, and Israel saw the Egyptians dead on the seashore. Israel saw the great power that the Lord used against the Egyptians, so the people feared the Lord, and they believed in the Lord, and in his servant, Moses."
~ Exodus 14:30-31

1. What is the hardest part of taking the first step in following God?

2. Why is walking by sight so much more attractive to the modern world?

3. How does knowing the wonders of God or reflecting on them boost your confidence and faith to live boldly when you come against obstacles in life?

Diving Deeper

1. What is the biggest takeaway from this passage?

2. What are some ways you could apply this passage?

3. When you face a crisis in the future, will you stand still knowing God is fighting for you? What can you do when fear tells you to retreat, or impatience tells you to do something now?

4. What will you apply specifically this week?

5. Who will hold you accountable this week for your response to Question 4?

"We are always on the anvil; by trials God is shaping us for higher things."
~ Henry Ward Beecher

🦶 GROW Passages for Week 4

1. Exodus 1:1-2:25

2. Exodus 3:1-4:17

3. Exodus 6:28-10:29

4. Exodus 11:1-12:51

5. Exodus 13:1-14:31

SESSION 5

The Idols of our Worship

Exodus 32:1-33:6

In an article, *"How to Talk About Sin in a Postmodern Age,"* Timothy Keller mentions the book, *Easter Everywhere* by Darcy Steinke. Keller recounts how Steinke, "the daughter of a Lutheran minister, left her Christian profession. Moving to New York City she entered a life of club hopping and sexual obsession. She wrote several novels. She continued, however, to be extremely restless and unfulfilled. In the middle of the book, she quotes from Simone Weill as summarizing the main issue in her life. "One has only the choice between God and idolatry; if one denies God ... one is worshiping some things of this world in the belief that one sees them only as such, but in fact, though unknown to oneself imagining the attributes of Divinity in them." Every human heart was designed to worship God. When a person substitutes God with something else, they continue to long for what they were designed to possess, the character of God.

Idolatry leaves one longing for something or someone real, tangible, communicative, and caring. Idols of man's imagination can offer nothing but emptiness and unfilled desire. In fact, that is the definition of hell's reality. Hell will be the eternal longing for self-satisfaction and self-fulfillment without the possibility of ever reaching it.

Christian worship is to be pure; not mixed with half-heartedness and loyalties for something set up to make God conform to our thoughts. Dallas Willard sums up insightfully the proper perspective of worship: "Human beings are at their core defined by what they worship rather than primarily by what they think, know, or believe. That is bound up with the central Augustinian claim that we are what we love." What we love will be evidenced in who and how we worship!

Connecting to the Story

Have you ever wondered if God listens to your prayers? Have you sometimes felt like it is a waste of time, that the heavens are closed to your prayers? What has been your biggest struggle in prayer?

Diving into the Story

What's It All About
Chapters 32-34 are an interlude between the blueprints of the tabernacle and the actual building process. Aaron, Moses' brother, falls into idolatry and orders the making of a golden calf, representative of an old pagan god from Egypt. This is a flagrant violation of God's commandments. When Moses becomes aware of this, he throws the tablets containing the Ten Commandments to the ground and burns the false god. Now Moses becomes more than the voice of God to the people, he becomes the voice of God on behalf of his followers.

The Big Idea
When Adam and Eve sinned in the Garden of Eden by not obeying God's command, they violated their trust in God and belief that as their Creator, He had authority over them and unconditionally cared for them. They substituted God's love for the thoughts of their imaginations, and they decided to become lovers of self rather than lovers of God. As a result, humanity made gods in their own image. They made idols to represent

their idea of how God should be and act. But in reality, they forfeited the beauty of God's glory for the ugliness of man's evil heart. Thus, separation from God created a massive divide and nothing can change it until the heart itself is transformed.

Christ in the Text

Exodus is a book of redemption. God's freeing His people from Egyptian slavery is a picture of Christ's delivering sinners from their sin and its consequences. Christ was with Israel as the rock that followed them through their journey from slavery to the promised land. The Passover Lambs are a picture of Christ's death for sinners and His providing access to God.

#1 Aaron's Sin (32:1-6)

When the people saw that Moses delayed to come down from the mountain, the people gathered themselves together to Aaron and said to him, "Up, make us gods who shall go before us. As for this Moses, the man who brought us up out of the land of Egypt, we do not know what has become of him." So Aaron said to them, "Take off the rings of gold that are in the ears of your wives, your sons, and your daughters, and bring them to me." So all the people took off the rings of gold that were in their ears and brought them to Aaron. And he received the gold from their hand and fashioned it with a graving tool and made a golden calf.

And they said, "These are your gods, O Israel, who brought you up out of the land of Egypt!" When Aaron saw this, he built an altar before it. And Aaron made a proclamation and said, "Tomorrow shall be a feast to the LORD." And they rose up early the next day and offered burnt offerings and brought peace offerings. And the people sat down to eat and drink and rose up to play.
~ Exodus 32:1-6

1. Why do people turn to idols? And, what are some idols we see in our culture today?

2. Which golden calves in our culture draw our loyalty and love away from God when we get impatient waiting on God?

2 The Glory of God (14:13-21)

The LORD said to Moses, "Depart; go up from here, you and the people whom you have brought up out of the land of Egypt, to the land of which I swore to Abraham, Isaac, and Jacob, saying, 'To your offspring I will give it.' I will send an angel before you, and I will drive out the Canaanites, the Amorites, the Hittites, the Perizzites, the Hivites, and the Jebusites. Go up to a land flowing with milk and honey; but I will not go up among you, lest I consume you on the way, for you are a stiff-necked people."

When the people heard this disastrous word, they mourned, and no one put on his ornaments. For the LORD had said to Moses, "Say to the people of Israel, 'You are a stiff-necked people; if for a single moment I should go up among you, I would consume you. So now take off your ornaments, that I may know what to do with you.'" Therefore, the people of Israel stripped themselves of their ornaments, from Mount Horeb onward.
~ Exodus 33:1-6

1. How do we maintain this story's delicate balance between divine judgment with consequences for disobedience along with God's dominant leaning toward mercy, forgiveness and faithfulness to the promises God has made?

2. What do you need to strip yourself from that could be keeping you from experiencing the glory of God?

ⓘ Diving Deeper

1. What is the biggest takeaway from this passage?

2. What are some ways you could apply this passage?

3. Have we made the God who we worship into an idol, a small, fixed statue, that we try to control and manipulate as a substitute for the free, untamed, mysterious, and surprising God of the universe, who will not be tied down to small and humanly constructed images, ideologies, institutions and idols?

4. What will you apply specifically this week?

5. Who will hold you accountable this week for your response to Question 4?

"We make a god out of whatever we find most joy in. So, find your joy in God and be done with all idolatry."

~ John Piper

🦶 GROW Passages for Week 5

1. Exodus 15:22-17:15

2. Exodus 19:1-20:26

3. Numbers 21:4-9

4. Exodus 32:1-33:6

5. Joshua 1:1-2:24; 5:13-6:27

SESSION 6

The Kinsman-Redeemer

Ruth 1-4

In their classic book, *Reconciling All Things: A Christian Vision for Justice, Peace and Healing*, authors Emmanuel Katongale and Chris Rice share a story about Billy Neal Moore and the reconciliation he experienced from the family of his murder victim. They write, "When Billy Neal Moore was in jail, awaiting the trial in which he would be sentenced to death, a minister shared with him the good news that Jesus loved him and wanted to forgive his sins. Moore learned that no one is beyond redemption. From prison, he wrote to his victim's family and asked their forgiveness.

Astoundingly, they immediately wrote back to say that they also were Christians and that they forgave him. Then the family decided to petition the Georgia parole board to commute Moore's death sentence. In 1991, Moore was paroled from prison, transformed by the grace of God and his victim's family members. 'When I was released, they embraced me like a brother,' Moore said of Stapleton's family. He has been preaching the gospel of forgiveness to schoolchildren and church groups ever since."

Stories of reconciliation warm out hearts and cause us to believe that all in our world is not lost. While much of the world sways under the pressures of greed, gossip, deception and suffering, there are those who have been captivated by a greater love than the world could ever know.

The love of Jesus, our Kinsman-Redeemer stands above the fray to announce to the world that all is not lost. As Kinsman-Redeemer, Jesus is the reconciler of men to God, and as a result, He makes it possible for God to commune with sinful man.

How? He has reconciled all things to Himself. Reconciliation is the heartbeat of the gospel. Without reconciliation, life is chaotic, violent, merciless, and unforgiving. However, God put within humanity a capacity to forgive that ultimately came from the only One who could bring reconciliation: Jesus Christ.

For all those who have been reconciled, He gives us the ministry of reconciliation (2 Cor. 5:18-20). There may be no better story to picture God's reconciliation than the story of Ruth and Boaz. In their story, we get a picture of Christ's great love and willingness to step in on our behalf to claim us as His own.

Connecting to the Story

The Book of Ruth is the eighth book in the Bible. In Biblical numerology, number eight stands for "New Beginnings." Have you ever driven down a new, unfamiliar road? Roads where the asphalt unravels like a secret in the wind. The unfamiliar bends and turns are all question marks of where it will lead us. Naomi and Ruth must have felt their road was leading to nowhere and eventually everywhere! For in their unfamiliar, they would find "New Beginnings!"

The days of the judges (Ruth 1:1) were turbulent times. Judges 21:25 tells us, "There was no king in the land, and everyone did what was right in his own sight." Anarchy ruled, and God disciplined His people through cycles of invasion, deliverance, and restoration.

It was during these invasions and the destruction of the land, that there was a famine in Judah. Even in Bethlehem—The House of Bread—people were suffering. Amidst this backdrop, the story of Ruth emerges revealing themes of kindness, redemption, and God's sovereignty.

👣 Diving into the Story

What's It All About
God Uses Unlikely People for His Purpose. Ruth is only one of two Books of the Bible named after women. Ruth is also one of a few women who are mentioned in the genealogy of Jesus found in Matthew's Gospel. And this was at a time when women were not usually included in genealogies. Ruth, a Moabite woman, became an essential character in a powerful story of salvation woven through the Bible.

Ruth's story is ordinary. Perhaps that's what makes it so compelling. She didn't come from a famous family. She did not have great riches or a great position. Ruth is just a widow – one from an enemy nation, at that. Nothing is going in her favor, but she's brave, and her faith never wavers. And yet the life of a foreign widow who has nothing becomes so important that it's included in the Bible and her name recognized in the lineage of Jesus.

God's voice never thunders down to her as you might read in other Bible stories. No earth-shattering miracles, like the Red Sea parting, happened in her life. But what you do see is an ordinary – and challenging – life shaped by faith and guided by the God she believed in, and today we can look back and see the mighty way her life was used.

Tragedy and Suffering. A famine in Canaan forced Elimelech and Naomi, along with their sons, to migrate from Bethlehem to Moab. Their sons married Moabite women, Orpah and Ruth. Elimelech passed away, and about 10 years later, both of Naomi's sons died, as well. Naomi, Ruth, and Orpah were all widows.

Loyalty and Devotion. Hearing that the Lord had come to the aid of His people back in Judah by providing them with food, Naomi decided to return home. She urged her daughters-in-law to go back to their mother's homes, expressing her hope that the Lord would show them kindness as they did to her. Initially, both women wished to accompany Naomi, but after insisting they have a better chance of finding new husbands and building families in their homeland, Orpah decided to leave. However, Ruth clung to Naomi, showing unwavering loyalty. Naomi encouraged Ruth to follow her sister-in-law, but Ruth made a profound and heartfelt pledge to Naomi. Ruth decided to go wherever Naomi went, live where Naomi lived, accept Naomi's people as her own, and Naomi's God as her God. Naomi, seeing Ruth's determination, stopped urging her.

Return to Bethlehem. Upon their return to Bethlehem, the town was excited, but Naomi asked them to call her "Mara" (meaning bitter), for she believed the Almighty had made her life very bitter. Naomi attributed her misfortunes to the Lord's hand against her. Despite her bitterness, everyone else experienced a hopeful note as it was the beginning of the barley harvest.

Divine Providence Led Ruth to Boaz's Field. In her pursuit of sustenance, Ruth, unaware of Boaz's relation to Naomi, found herself in his field to glean grain. While she was there, Boaz arrived from Bethlehem and, observing the unfamiliar face of Ruth in his field, asked about her. His servants informed him of Ruth's identity and her commitment to his kin, Naomi.

Boaz's Kindness and Generosity. Boaz generously allowed Ruth to glean in his fields, providing her protection and allowing her to share his workers' water. He also invited her to eat with his workers, personally giving her roasted grain. Ruth was treated with kindness and respect, despite being a foreigner.

Ruth's Devotion and Naomi's Recognition. Ruth worked diligently and returned home to share her bounty and recount her day to Naomi. Naomi identified Boaz as a close relative, one with the power to redeem them. She advised Ruth to stay with Boaz's female servants and glean from his field until the end of the barley and wheat harvests.

Naomi's Plan. Naomi, in her wisdom and concern for Ruth's future, came up with a plan for Ruth to approach Boaz, their kinsman, and possible redeemer, at the threshing floor. She advised Ruth on how to present herself and when to approach Boaz. Ruth agreed to follow Naomi's instructions.

Ruth on the Threshing Floor. Ruth did as Naomi instructed and waited until Boaz was asleep and then lay down at his feet. Startled in the middle of the night, Boaz discovered Ruth. She boldly asked him to spread his garment over—a symbolic request for marriage.

The Big Idea

Throughout the Bible, we see previews of Christ. In the book of Ruth, we see Boaz as a "type" of Christ – he's the "redeemer" of Ruth. These previews of Christ are a bit of a "foreshadowing" that falls across Old Testament pages, fully coming to reality in the New Testament with the birth of Jesus. While Boaz was a "kinsman redeemer," when Jesus came to earth as a man, he became our "kinsman redeemer" in the flesh. Boaz redeemed Ruth, but years later Jesus became the "redeemer" of mankind.

Christ in the Text

Jesus Christ is our "kinsman redeemer," who paid the price for us and satisfied our debt so that we would not lose our inheritance. Romans 8:17 tells us that we are brothers and sisters in Christ and heirs together to the throne—that means He is our brother. Jesus is our nearest relative. Sin has separated us from the Father leaving us orphans, much like Naomi and Ruth were left alone in Moab. So, Jesus came to be our kinsman-redeemer. Through His shed blood on the cross, He has bought us our freedom and restored our relationship with the Father.

#1 God's Plan in Unexpected Situations (3:10-13)

And he said, "May you be blessed by the LORD, my daughter. You have made this last kindness greater than the first in that you have not gone after young men, whether poor or rich. And now, my daughter, do not fear. I will do for you all that you ask, for all my fellow townsmen know that you are a worthy woman. And now it is true that I am a redeemer. Yet there is a redeemer nearer than I. Remain tonight, and in the morning, if he will redeem you, good; let him do it. But if he is not willing to redeem you, then, as the LORD lives, I will redeem you. Lie down until the morning."
~ *Ruth 3:10-13*

1. What did Ruth's boldness teach about stepping out of our comfort zone in faith?

2. How did Boaz's response reflect God's loving-kindness?

3. How did Boaz demonstrate integrity and honor in this situation?

2 God's Plan Includes Kinsman-Redeemer Laws (4:1-10)

Now Boaz had gone up to the gate and sat down there. And behold, the redeemer, of whom Boaz had spoken, came by. So Boaz said, "Turn aside, friend; sit down here." And he turned aside and sat down. And he took ten men of the elders of the city and said, "Sit down here." So they sat down. ³ Then he said to the redeemer, "Naomi, who has come back from the country of Moab, is selling the parcel of land that belonged to our relative Elimelech.

So I thought I would tell you of it and say, 'Buy it in the presence of those sitting here and in the presence of the elders of my people.' If you will redeem it, redeem it. But if you will not, tell me, that I may know, for there is no one besides you to redeem it, and I come after you." And he said, "I will redeem it." Then Boaz said, "The day you buy the field from the hand of Naomi, you also acquire Ruth the Moabite, the widow of the dead, in order to perpetuate the name of the dead in his inheritance." Then the redeemer said, "I cannot redeem it for myself, lest I impair my own inheritance. Take my right of redemption yourself, for I cannot redeem it."

Now this was the custom in former times in Israel concerning redeeming and exchanging: to confirm a transaction, the one drew off his sandal and gave it to the other, and this was the manner of attesting in Israel. So when the redeemer said to Boaz, "Buy it for yourself," he drew off his sandal. Then Boaz said to the elders and all the people, "You are witnesses this day that I have bought from the hand of Naomi all that belonged to Elimelech and all that belonged to Chilion and to Mahlon. Also Ruth the Moabite, the widow of Mahlon, I have bought to be my wife, to perpetuate the name of the dead in his inheritance, that the name of the dead may not be cut off from among his brothers and from the gate of his native place.
You are witnesses this day."
*~ **Ruth 4:1-10***

1. How was the virtue and character of Boaz displayed in his interactions with Ruth and the closer relative?

2. How did the theme of God's Providence unfold in this passage?

3 God's Providential Care (4:13-21)

So Boaz took Ruth, and she became his wife. And he went in to her, and the LORD gave her conception, and she bore a son. Then the women said to Naomi, "Blessed be the LORD, who has not left you this day without a redeemer, and may his name be renowned in Israel!

He shall be to you a restorer of life and a nourisher of your old age, for your daughter-in-law who loves you, who is more to you than seven sons, has given birth to him." Then Naomi took the child and laid him on her lap and became his nurse. And the women of the neighborhood gave him a name, saying, "A son has been born to Naomi."

They named him Obed. He was the father of Jesse, the father of David. Now these are the generations of Perez: Perez fathered Hezron, Hezron fathered Ram, Ram fathered Amminadab, Amminadab fathered Nahshon, Nahshon fathered Salmon, Salmon fathered Boaz, Boaz fathered Obed, Obed fathered Jesse, and Jesse fathered David."
~ Ruth 4:13-21

1. What significance does the lineage of King David hold in the larger biblical narrative?

2. How did Naomi's life change throughout the story, and what role did Ruth play in this transformation?

❾ Diving Deeper

1. What is the biggest takeaway from this passage?

2. What are some ways you could apply this passage?

3. What will you apply specifically this week?

4. Who will hold you accountable this week for your response to Question 3?

"The cost of redemption cannot be overstated. The wonders of grace cannot be overemphasized. Christ took the hell He didn't deserve so we could have the heaven we don't deserve."

~ Randy Alcorn

👣 GROW Passages for Week 6

1. Joshua 7:1-8:29

2. Judges 6:1-7:25

3. Judges 13:1-16:31

4. Ruth 1:1-4:22

5. 1 Samuel 1:1-3:21

SESSION 7

No Giant is Too Big

1 Samuel 17:1-58

"Houston, we have a problem." On April 14, 1970, the astronauts on the NASA Apollo 13 mission to the moon experienced an explosion. Command module pilot, Jack Swigert said, "Okay, Houston, we've had a problem here." Mission Control in Houston asked for the crew to repeat what they said. Mission Commander, Jim Lovell, responded, "Ah, Houston...we've had a problem." At least, that was the exact line given by the crew. The problem on board was gigantic and life threatening. The entire country waited to see if the astronauts would make it safely home. As the hours went by, NASA engineers used rudimentary technology (less than what is in a cell phone) to figure out a way for the crew to return home. On April 17, 1970 the crew splashed down safely in the Pacific. Both the crew of Apollo 13 and the engineers had a massive problem to solve, and they did it together. In the 1995 movie version, *Apollo 13*, the NASA Director said, "This could be the worst disaster NASA has ever experienced." Without batting an eye, Gene Kranz, NASA Flight Director responded, "With all due respect sir, I believe this is going to be our finest hour."

Many times, in life, you face situations beyond your understanding to solve. You face a financial giant due to a job loss, or a family crisis due to sickness or death. Rebellious children, marital conflicts, mental health struggles and the stressful decisions of life create these massive giants striking fear in your hearts and minds.

One day everything is going along great and the next you are standing in front of this massive giant frozen with uncertainty, anxiety, dread and discouragement. A young David, the future king of Israel, walked onto the battle field to simply resupply his brothers with food, but became a national hero, because for David, no giant was too big for his God to conquer. As David confidently faced Goliath, we have to learn the lessons David demonstrated when he stood before his giant.

In this most familiar story, we learn that when your faith stands in God, no giant can stand against you. You might be facing some massive problems in your life, but nothing is too big for God. He conquered the greatest giant of all when Jesus died for your sins and defeated death through His resurrection. Therefore, you can trust Him, delight in Him and know He is able to take down any giant you face. Are you ready to see your giants fall?

Connecting to the Story

Why has the story of David and Goliath been told so often? What is it about the story that fascinates you and challenges you?

Diving into the Story

What's It All About
The story of David and Goliath is not merely the story of an underdog courageously rising against an ominous oppressor in victory, but it serves as a metaphor about the challenges of life and how people can overcome them. David's battle with Goliath demonstrates faith that every Christian needs when faced with the realities of life's difficult moments that loom large over them. The metaphor of giants being the manifestations of overwhelming trials is certainly an application made consistently by pastors, theologians and writers for centuries, but the point of the story is God's power in using a young boy, without dependency on anything except God, to defeat an enemy who openly opposed the living God and defied God's people. God's name was on the line, and David was not about to allow this uncircumcised Philistine to drag God's name through

the mud. Neither should any Christian! The name of the Lord is sacred and holy. His name is righteous and must be honored. David would do whatever it took to make sure everyone in that valley and encamped on the hillsides knew "that the Lord saves not with sword and spear...For the battle is the Lord's" (1 Sam. 17:47).

There was no giant big enough to defeat God's people. They had survived hundreds of years in slavery, escaped the pursuing army of Egypt, watched as God delivered them across the Red Sea, provided food in the desert, led them into the Promised Land, and defeated nation after nation to move them prosperously into the land of their inheritance. Would this giant of a man be able to stop them? It would seem so. All of Israel's armies cowered in their barracks and camps for over 40 days with Goliath taunting them every day; until one young man, filled with the Spirit and empowered with conviction that God alone was enough, stepped up and took on the giant. David did not allow the externals to dictate reality. He believed as John would later say, "Greater is he who is in me, than he that is in the world" (1 John 4:4).

David faced an intimidating enemy with confidence in his identity in Christ which enabled him to respond in fearless faith. Knowing *who* you are and *whose* you are empowers you with fearlessness to take on every adversity with victorious faith. This story is not only a story for children's books, but the story for every person who faces intimidating giants trying to wreck your faith and cause you to cower away from the battles ahead. David knew the power of God was enough. Now, God's people have to know it too, and they have to stand in his power to experience victory.

The power to face your enemy is not found within. You are not the solution to all your problems. You may contribute to them and make them worse, but you can dig, educate or problem-solve your way out to victory. When Goliath stepped out on the battlefield, he said, "Give me a man!" Our giants do not look to fight against everyone, just one! You! And you are not able to win on your own. Your family, your church, you, need a representative to fight for you! As Alan Redpath clearly articulates, "Here we get a glimpse into the basic fact of the Bible, for the whole issue is not the devil arrayed against a multitude of Christian people – it is the devil against God! It is Satan versus Jesus! And the whole issue is basically settled, not only in the life of a church, but in the life of a Christian, by our Representative. What happens to the prince of the power of darkness happens to all who follow him. What happens to our Lord, David's greater Son, happens to all who follow him. David here is a picture of the Lord Jesus Christ, who overcame Satan at Calvary, and also a picture of every child of God who is being made one with him through faith and obedience. Christ is the head and we are his body, and therefore, if He has won the victory over Satan, so have we. How pointless would be any series of Bible studies unless we caught a fresh glimpse of the loveliness of our Lord Jesus Christ!"

The Big Idea

Every day you face moments that test your character and faith. These tests could be the result of poor choices that cause you to confront severe consequences, while other tests are the work of God to strengthen your faith for greater challenges ahead. Giants intimidate with shame, guilt and fear, but no matter how intimidating your problems may seem, there is nothing too big when you stand with confidence and fearless faith in the One who gives you the power to slay ever giant you face.

Christ in the Text

Jesus came to deliver you from all enemies who threaten our freedom, allowing you to stand with confidence in your identity in Him and with fearless faith in every situation.

#1 No Giant is Too Big When You Face Intimidating Attacks from the Enemy (17:1-23)

Now the Philistines gathered their armies for battle. And they were gathered at Socoh, which belongs to Judah, and encamped between Socoh and Azekah, in Ephes-dammim. And Saul and the men of Israel were gathered, and encamped in the Valley of Elah, and drew up in line of battle against the Philistines. And the Philistines stood on the mountain on the one side, and Israel stood on the mountain on the other side, with a valley between them.

And there came out from the camp of the Philistines a champion named Goliath of Gath, whose height was six cubits and a span. He had a helmet of bronze on his head, and he was armed with a coat of mail, and the weight of the coat was five thousand shekels of bronze. And he had bronze armor on his legs, and a javelin of bronze slung between his shoulders. The shaft of his spear was like a weaver's beam, and his spear's head weighed six hundred shekels of iron.

And his shield-bearer went before him. He stood and shouted to the ranks of Israel,
"Why have you come out to draw up for battle? Am I not a Philistine, and are you
not servants of Saul? Choose a man for yourselves, and let him come down to me. If he
is able to fight with me and kill me, then we will be your servants. But if I prevail
against him and kill him, then you shall be our servants and serve us." And the
Philistine said, "I defy the ranks of Israel this day. Give me a man, that we may fight
together." When Saul and all Israel heard these words
of the Philistine, they were dismayed and greatly afraid.
~ 1 Samuel 17:1-11(12-23)

1. What are some "giants" you are facing now or have faced recently?

2. How have they intimidated you in the past?

3. What should we "know" that should keep us from succumbing to our fears when giants come on the attack?

2 No Giant is Too Big When You Stand in the Confidence of Your Identity in Christ (17:24-47)

"When the words that David spoke were heard, they repeated them before Saul, and
he sent for him. And David said to Saul, "Let no man's heart fail because of
him. Your servant will go and fight with this Philistine."
And Saul said to David, "You are not able to go against this Philistine to fight with
him, for you are but a youth, and he has been a man of war from his youth." But
David said to Saul, "Your servant used to keep sheep for his father. And when there
came a lion, or a bear, and took a lamb from the flock, I went after him and struck
him and delivered it out of his mouth. And if he arose against me, I caught him by his
beard and struck him and killed him.

Your servant has struck down both lions and bears, and this uncircumcised Philistine shall be like one of them, for he has defied the armies of the living God." And David said, "The LORD who delivered me from the paw of the lion and from the paw of the bear will deliver me from the hand of this Philistine." And Saul said to David, "Go, and the LORD be with you!"

Then David said to the Philistine, "You come to me with a sword and with a spear and with a javelin, but I come to you in the name of the LORD of hosts, the God of the armies of Israel, whom you have defied.
~ 1 Samuel 17:31-37, 45 (24-47)

1. How do you handle ridicule from others? How did David?

2. What lessons can we learn from David's faith to help us face our problems, not with the resources of the flesh but in dependence of the Spirit?

3 No Giant is Too Big When You Respond with Fearless Faith to Your Adversity (17:48-58)

When the Philistine arose and came and drew near to meet David, David ran quickly toward the battle line to meet the Philistine. And David put his hand in his bag and took out a stone and slung it and struck the Philistine on his forehead. The stone sank into his forehead, and he fell on his face to the ground.
So David prevailed over the Philistine with a sling and with a stone, and struck the Philistine and killed him. There was no sword in the hand of David. Then David ran and stood over the Philistine and took his sword and drew it out of its sheath and killed him and cut off his head with it. When the Philistines saw that their champion was dead, they fled. And the men of Israel and Judah rose with a shout and pursued the Philistines as far as Gath and the gates of Ekron, so that the wounded Philistines fell on the way from Shaaraim as far as Gath and Ekron. And the people of Israel came back from chasing the Philistines, and they plundered their camp.

And David took the head of the Philistine and brought it to Jerusalem, but he put his armor in his tent. As soon as Saul saw David go out against the Philistine, he said to Abner, the commander of the army, "Abner, whose son is this youth?" And Abner said, "As your soul lives, O king, I do not know." And the king said, "Inquire whose son the boy is." And as soon as David returned from the striking down of the Philistine, Abner took him, and brought him before Saul with the head of the Philistine in his hand. And Saul said to him, "Whose son are you, young man?" And David answered, "I am the son of your servant Jesse the Bethlehemite."
~ 1 Samuel 17:48-58

1. When is the last time you faced a giant in your life? How did it go?

2. What lessons did you learn?

3. What lessons from David's experience can help you grow with fearless faith?

🦶 Diving Deeper

1. What is the biggest takeaway from this passage?

2. What are some ways you could apply this passage?

3. What will you apply specifically this week?

4. Who will hold you accountable this week for your response to Question 3?

"If you try to tackle the giant in the flesh, you cannot get it done. You'll lose.
But when you have spent sufficient time on your knees,
it's remarkable how stable you can be."
~ **Charles Swindoll**

GROW Passages for Week 7

1. 1 Samuel 8:1-10:26

2. 1 Samuel 16:1-23

3. 1 Samuel 17:1-58

4. 2 Samuel 11:1-12:31; Psalm 51

5. 1 Kings 3:1-28

SESSION 8

The Lord is My Shepherd

Psalm 23:1-6

Psalm 23 may be the most familiar and read chapter in the bible. The six verses encapsulate the heart of God as our Shepherd, His guidance through the valleys of life, correction when we stray to dangerous places, and assurance provided to us an eternal home with Him. This passage has comforted families grieving over a loss, guided people through times of fear and provided hope when life seemed hopeless. Pastor Tony Evans writes, "Most of us have experienced our children's dependence on us to face their fears when they have nightmares or when it's thundering and lightning during a storm.

They'll wake up, scream, and jump out of their bed. They will walk through the valley of their bedroom, down the valley of their hall, to the valley of your room. They jump in your bed, because what they need is somebody to be with them. Your hugging them doesn't stop the rain, thunder, or the lightning, but it changes how they face it. They'll fall asleep in your arms. The fear that they have alone, they no longer have, because Mama and Daddy hold them. You help them face their fears in the midst of their struggles. This is exactly what the heavenly Father does for us when we face our own fears and insecurities." What insecurities do you face each day? How can the Lord, your Shepherd guide you through the valleys in your life?

In this lesson, you will discover how the Lord is your help to bring calm and peace to your troubled soul. He is your hope when you walk through the most difficult seasons of life, and the Lord is your home because you have in Him ultimate and eternal rest. The beauty of Psalm 23 is not in the comfort it brings people in times of grieving, but the grandeur of seeing the Lord as the only One who is able to give us help, hope and home to souls vexed by the devastating realities of sin.

As A.W. Tozer writes, "Were all human beings suddenly to become blind, still the sun would shine by day and the stars by night, for these owe nothing to the millions who benefit from their light. So, were every man on earth to be an atheist, it could not affect God in any way. He is what He is in Himself without regard to any other. To believe in Him adds nothing to His perfections; to doubt Him takes nothing away." Such is the beauty of the Lord our Shepherd!

 # Connecting to the Story

What is your favorite part of Psalm 23? How has it impacted your life?

Diving into the Story

What's It All About

Psalm 23 is no doubt the most famous and read chapter in the Bible. In English it covers six verses, 113 words (ESV) and divides beautifully into three sections. Henry Ward Beecher writes, "David has left no sweeter Psalm than the twenty-third. It is but a moment's opening of his soul; but, as when one, walking the winter street, sees the door opened for someone to enter, and the red light streams a moment forth, and the forms of gay children are running to greet the comer, and the genial music sounds, though the doors shuts and leaves the night black, yet it cannot shut back again all that the eyes, the ear, the heart, and the imagination have seen – so in this Psalm is the nightingale of the Psalms."

The twenty-third Psalm is David's personal biography. His opening line, "the Lord is my shepherd," points to his identity. The Lord is the one guiding, protecting, providing and correcting his steps. In these simple and concise verses, the life of every Christian is described. The Lord who is our shepherd provides so ably for His sheep that they have plenteous help for every need. The intentionality of the Lord communicates His unending provisions, careful guidance to places of spiritual nourishment, leadership to springs of living water, restoration for the soul and God-honoring leadership to a life fully pleasing to Him. And that is only His help!

The Lord our Shepherd is our hope as we walk through the treacherous hillsides, mountains and valleys of life where death is looming and evil seeks to lure us off the paths of righteousness. God is always with us with His staff of guidance and rod of correction. When Christians rest in their Good Shepherd, there is no fear. Hope in Christ overpowers the fear of failure, rejection, abandonment or judgment. The Lord provides confidence to move through valleys of danger and see the truth about reality. He provides security with His presence in the face of death. He is our hope!

Finally, the Lord our Shepherd is our home. Dwelling in the house of the Lord is the place of deepest refuge. Through the Lord providing protection from the poisonous ways of the believer's enemies, He supplies healing that leads to joy which follows His people from life into eternity.

This Psalm gives assurance of everything God's people need to experience security, peace, joy and love. It confronts the enemy, Satan, with the help of the Shepherd and assures us with the knowledge that we are safe from all harm. There is no Psalm that gets to the heart of all Christians like that of Psalm 23.

The Big Idea

People search constantly for purpose and significance for their life, and they live with nagging dissatisfaction because they have put their trust in people, possessions and philosophies that cannot provide for what their soul desperately needs. Every soul needs the Shepherd who patiently guides His sheep to pastures of satisfying provision. When the Lord is your Shepherd, He is your help, hope, and home for a life lived with security and satisfaction.

Christ in the Text

Jesus is the Good Shepherd who leads, walks, protects and prepares you for every moment in life so that you find in Him your help, hope and home in this life and eternity.

#1 The Lord is My Help (Psalm 23:1-3)

"The Lord is my shepherd; I shall not want. He makes me lie down in green pastures. He leads me beside still waters. He restores my soul. He leads me in the paths of righteousness for his name's sake."
~ Psalm 23:1-3

1. What are some parallels between sheep and people?

2. What are some specific areas of your life in which you need "extra" help?

2 The Lord is My Hope (23:4)

"Even though I walk through the valley of the shadow of death, I will fear no evil, for you are with me;
your rod and your staff, they comfort me."
~ Psalm 23:4

1. What are your deepest fears?

2. How does this verse influence the way you face your fears?

3. In what ways have you experienced the Lord's rod and staff guiding and protecting you?

3 The Lord is My Home (23:5-6)

"You prepare a table before me in the presence of my enemies; you anoint my head with oil; my cup overflows. Surely goodness and mercy shall follow me all the days of my life, and I shall dwell in the house of the Lord forever."
~ Psalm 23:5-6

1. Describe home. Was it a positive or negative place for you?

2. How do David's words about being at rest help to give you a better sense of 'home'?

3. How do these verses impact the way you live life now when the trials of life press hard against you?

🐾 Diving Deeper

1. What is the biggest takeaway from this passage?

2. What are some ways you could apply this passage?

3. In his book, *Don't Give the Enemy a Seat at Your Table*, Louie Giglio writes, "The Devil wants nothing more than to crush you. He wants to steal from you everything you value. He wants to kill everything in your life that's good. Ultimately, he wants to destroy you. If he can claim the victory over your mind, he can eventually claim the victory over your life. But the message of Psalm 23 is that the Good Shepherd prepares a table for you. It's a table for two, and the Devil is not invited to sit." Has there been a time when you gave Satan a seat at your table (in the affairs of your life)? How can you resist his insistence to be invited in?

4. What will you apply specifically this week?

"Let us go on believing, and not be afraid. It is everything to be a real Christian. None have such a King, such a Priest, such a constant Companion, and such an unfailing Friend, as the true servants of Christ."
~ **J.C. Ryle**

🦶 GROW Passages for Week 8

1. Psalm 1:1-6

2. Psalm 23:1-6

3. Psalm 139:1-24

4. Proverbs 3:1-12

5. 1 Kings 17:1-24; 18:16-46

SESSION 9

Who Do You Love?

Jonah 1-4

In his book, *Grace for Giving*, Stephen Olford tells of a Baptist pastor, Peter Miller, who pastored in Ephrata, Pennsylvania during the American Revolution. Miller enjoyed a longtime friendship with General George Washington. Miller's most ardent antagonist in Ephrata was an evil-minded man named Michael Wittman. One day Michael Wittman was arrested for treason and sentenced to die. Peter Miller traveled seventy miles on foot to Philadelphia to plead for the life of the traitor. "No, Peter," General Washington said. "I cannot grant you the life of your friend." "My friend!" exclaimed the old preacher. "He's the bitterest enemy I have."

"What?" cried Washington. "You've walked seventy miles to save the life of an enemy? That puts the matter in a different light. I'll grant your pardon." And he did. Peter Miller took Michael Wittman back home to Ephrata--no longer an enemy but a friend.

The overarching message of the bible is the love of God. You see it in every act of mercy, grace and discipline. God not only loves His creation, but He puts His love in the human heart so everyone can experience knowing Him and loving others. The ability to love others is the most miraculous gift outside of Christ's demonstration of love through His death.

To love people is to experience the height of human emotion. But, when we fail to love others based on prejudice, race, social status, personality, outward appearance or personal biases, we reflect a sinful nature inherited from the beginning when man chose to live without God. When we fail to love, we fail to live as God created. In our sinful humanity, we love based on people who love us in return.

We tend to hate those who hate us, abuse us, offer us nothing in return or treat us unfairly. Barriers go up and relationships dissolve or are never established. In the story of Jonah, the prejudices and biases of the human heart are on full display. Jonah wants God to love him and provide for him as long as God acts the way Jonah thinks is right. Jonah does not want God to love all people, only those whom Jonah thinks deserve love.

The story ends with Jonah pouting and God probing Jonah's heart for answers. Who do you love? Do you love others conditionally? Do you expect God to love only those whom you believe deserve love? What are the areas of your heart that need to be examined as you study Jonah's story one more time?

Connecting to the Story

(1) As you grew up, were there some big moments where you rebelled against your parents? How did that go?

(2) What have been some effective forms of discipline you have seen or experienced?

Diving into the Story

What's It All About

Jonah is listed among the minor prophets mentioned in 2 Kings 14:25 where Jonah is described as the son of Amittai, from Gath-hepher. Jonah helped expand the border of Israel in the north for the sake of Israel's protection. The book was written somewhere in the 5th or 4th century after the Babylonian exile. The verification of Jonah's historicity and story is the fact that Jesus mentions Jonah in response to the Pharisee's demand for a sign (Matthew 12:38-42).

The Book of Jonah divides into four chapters or four scenes. Jonah is the most unique story in the Old Testament among all the minor prophets. The other Old Testament prophets come on the scene with a message from God, meet resistance and continue to declare truth. Little is known about most prophets, with the brief exception of Hosea in chapters 1-3, but Jonah is a personal story of adventure, intrigue and reflection. Jonah comes out of nowhere, like most prophets, but called to a people the Israelites hate.

Not only do they hate them for their violence, pagan idolatry and evil practices, but Nineveh is a major threat to Northern Israel. Nineveh is the capital city of the Assyrian Empire. They were responsible for the destruction of the northern kingdom of Israel (2 Kings 17:1-23). Ninevites were a particularly violent nation who would drag their enemies through the sand with hooks going into their sinus captivity and through the bone at the bridge of the nose. They were also known to bury their enemies on the sand vertically, exposing their heads only, torturing them in the desert sun and exposing them to the birds of prey without the possibility of resistance. Desmond Alexander writes, "This explains Jonah's antipathy for Nineveh; he perceives the eventual outcome of his mission and passionately feels that he cannot be party to something that would ultimately mean the destruction of his own nation."

From the moment of God's revelation to Abraham, God moves through history with a single group of people who eventually become the nation of Israel. After Solomon's reign, Israel's third king, the kingdom is divides into two kingdoms, Israel in the north and Judea in the south. The history of the kingdoms is somewhat ignominious with both kingdoms struggling with idolatrous kings and halfhearted worshipers. The original design and purpose for God's people are lost to their compromise. God's purpose had always been for them to be God's light in the world. Instead, there was dim glimmer shining from a remnant of people in both kingdoms. After coming out of captivity to Babylon and then Assyria, Israel has the opportunity to rekindle their flame as they return to Jerusalem to rebuild the walls. Would they shine brightly or fall back into old habits? The Book of Jonah is a story from the life of an obscure prophet used to highlight the heart of God and expose Israel once again to the kind of people God wanted them to be.

From the outset of the book, Jonah illustrates the heart of God's people: still struggling to love like He does, still prejudiced against outsiders, still wanting justice at all costs, and still selfishly absorbed. The story of Jonah magnifies the unbelievable love of God for both religious rebels and irreligious pagans. God's mercy, grace and love shine brightly through Jonah's unapologetic aversion to share God's love with people he hated.

It also shines through the immediate repentance of a nation in the crosshairs of God's judgment, who up to this point, wants nothing to do with God. And yet, what the reader sees is the clear picture of what God does hundreds of years later when He breaks into human history as a baby, lives a picture-perfect life and freely lays down His life so every person who comes to Him by faith finds total and unconditional deliverance from their sin.

The book's purpose is not to simply provide a foreshadowing of God's redemptive plan, but to ask the question: Who do you really love? Does Jonah love a plant more than people for whom He came to save? Does Jonah only love those who agree with him, live like him or belong to his community? Will Jonah preach truth only to see God's judgment? Can Jonah submit his rage and disdain to the Lord and see the Ninevites from God's perspective? These are the questions every Christ follower must ask themselves.

If Christians walk away from this book unmoved, unconvinced or unrepentant, then they will walk away in the spirit of Jonah. But, if the Christian reader finds their heart stirred to radical change and begins to operate their lives with the compassion, mercy, grace and love found perfectly in Jesus Christ, then they will have learned God's purpose for including this wonderful story in His Holy Word.

The Big Idea

Every person, religious or irreligious, is loved by God as evidenced in His general care for them, but mainly, His redemptive work on the cross. He calls those who believe in Him to exemplify His love toward others too, no matter who they are, where they are or what they have done.

Christ in the Text

The story of Jonah is one of love and grace demonstrated to a rebellious prophet and a wicked nation. God's redemptive love is no respecter of persons, and His love for the religiously and irreligiously lost is found in the same expression of compassion through the work of Jesus Christ. Therefore, all those who come to faith in Christ live to express Christ's love to every person, no matter how deserving or undeserving they may be.

#1 Resistance (Jonah 1)

"Now the word of the LORD came to Jonah the son of Amittai, saying, "Arise, go to Nineveh, that great city, and call out against it, for their evil has come up before me." But Jonah rose to flee to Tarshish from the presence of the LORD. He went down to Joppa and found a ship going to Tarshish. So he paid the fare and went down into it, to go with them to Tarshish, away from the presence of the LORD."
~ Jonah 1:1-3 (1:1-17)

1. What is at the core of a Christian's decision to resist God's commands?

2. How does prejudice continue to rear its head even in the church?

3. What must the Christian's stance on racism, ethnic diversity and social justice be in light of God's call to make disciples of all nations?

2 Response (Jonah 2)

"Then Jonah prayed to the Lord his God from the belly of the fish…And the Lord spoke to the fish, and it vomited Jonah out on dry land."
~ Jonah 2:1, 10 (2:1-10)

1. What benefit was Jonah's recounting of his time in the sea to his prayer of thanksgiving?

2. What does Jonah's prayer teach you about God?

3. How could it change the way you pray?

3 Repentance (Jonah 3)

"Then the word of the LORD came to Jonah the second time, saying, "Arise, go to Nineveh, that great city, and call out against it the message that I tell you." So Jonah arose and went to Nineveh, according to the word of the LORD. Now Nineveh was an exceedingly great city, three days' journey in breadth. Jonah began to go into the city, going a day's journey. And he called out, "Yet forty days, and Nineveh shall be overthrown!" And the people of Nineveh believed God. They called for a fast and put on sackcloth, from the greatest of them to the least of them." When God saw what they did, how they turned from their evil way, God relented of the disaster that he had said he would do to them, and he did not do it."
~ Jonah 3:1-5, 10 (3:1-10)

1. What is the evidence of God's kindness in a world that rejects Him?

2. Read Acts 17:22-27. How does this passage fit within the Ninevite's repentance and what God wants to do through it in our world?

4 Reflection (Jonah 4)

"But it displeased Jonah exceedingly, and he was angry. And he prayed to the LORD and said, "O LORD, is not this what I said when I was yet in my country? That is why I made haste to flee to Tarshish; for I knew that you are a gracious God and merciful, slow to anger and abounding in steadfast love, and relenting from disaster. Therefore now, O LORD, please take my life from me, for it is better for me to die than to live." And the LORD said, "Do you do well to be angry?"
And the LORD said, "You pity the plant, for which you did not labor, nor did you make it grow, which came into being in a night and perished in a night. And should not I pity Nineveh, that great city, in which there are more than 120,000 persons who do not know their right hand from their left, and also much cattle?"
~ Jonah 4:1-4, 10-11 (4:1-11)

1. Who are the hardest people for you to love?

2. What are you going to do about this?

🦶 Diving Deeper

1. What is the biggest takeaway from this passage?

2. What are some ways you could apply this passage?

3. What is the biggest lesson in the Book of Jonah?

4. What will you apply specifically this week?

"God loves each one of us as if there were only one of us to love."
~ Augustine

🦶 GROW Passages for Week 9

1. Isaiah 6:1-13

2. Isaiah 53:1-12

3. Daniel 3:1-30

4. Daniel 6:1-28

5. Jonah 1 - 4

SESSION 10

Jesus is the One and Only

John 14:1-15:17

No one has impacted human history as much as Jesus Christ. People have believed in Him, lived their lives for Him, spent their life's fortune to share Him with the world and given their life's blood, because they knew He was the Son of God. No one can compare, and no one dare compares Jesus with anyone. He is unparalleled in His influence, perfection, character and compassion.

His virtues aside, what Jesus did through His death, burial and resurrection can never be matched. And yet, there is more! In his book, *The Radical Disciple*, John Stott writes, "We must continue to affirm the uniqueness and finality of Jesus Christ. For he is unique in his incarnation (the one and only God-man), unique in his atonement (only he has died for the sins of the world), and unique in his resurrection (only he has conquered death). And since in no other person but Jesus of Nazareth did God first become human (in his birth), then bear our sins (in his death), and then triumph over death (in his resurrection), he is uniquely competent to save sinners. Nobody else possesses his qualifications.

So we may talk about Alexander the Great, Charles the Great and Napoleon the Great, but not Jesus the Great. He is not the Great—he is the Only. There is nobody like him. He has no rival and no successor."

In Jesus' deity and humanity, you have the only source of true freedom and deliverance. He sets you free from your sin and delivers you from the penalty of God's wrath. For these reasons, Jesus is the source of our life as the True Vine through which flows the power of God to believe. By faith, you believe that he has not orphaned you but adopted you into His family. You know that He is the way, truth and the life.

Nothing is left to chance. If it is not Jesus, then you know that no one in all of creation can stand worthy. But knowing that it is Jesus who is the One and Only, you give your life for him! You stand with the saints from all time to proclaim the deity, majesty, righteousness and worthiness of the One who knew no sin but became sin so that you might become the righteousness of God in Christ Jesus (2 Cor. 5:21). On this fact, we live and breathe for Christ to be magnified in our lives.

Connecting to the Story

What are your phobias? Why is conquering fears liberating in the human experience?

Diving into the Story

What's It All About

As Jesus closes His ministry and heads toward His crucifixion, He gathers the disciples for final instructions. In John 13, Jesus washes their feet modeling a life of strength through humility. He then gives them a new commandment to love one another.

Then, as the men are in awe of each moment in the Upper Room, Jesus perceives their fear. He knows they will be tempted to scatter after his horrific death. Many of them will hide believing their life to be in danger by association.

The disciples have been with Jesus for over three years, and now he tells them that He will be leaving them. To assure their hearts and give them final instructions about life after He leaves, Jesus speaks the words of John 14 and 15.

This passage is rich in theology and practical Christian living. In essence, He lays out for them four applications they must carry with them if they are going to live fruitfully but also be the witness of Jesus, the One and Only Savior and Lord to the world:

(1) Jesus is the only Way, Truth and Life. Believe in the Lord Jesus who is in the Father and the Father in Him.
(2) Trust the Holy Spirit to be your counselor and teacher.
(3) Expect God's grace to calm your heart in troubled times.
(4) Remain in Christ and His word to be found faithful.

Each of these applications are seen in Christ's teaching. They shed light on the depth of His love for them and all those who believe in Him. Jesus is the One and Only who supersedes all others in His perfection, obedience, character and conduct. Without Jesus, there is no way to Heaven, no truth to know and no life to experience.

As C.H. Spurgeon said, "Without Jesus you can talk any quantity; but without him you can do nothing. The most eloquent discourse without him will be all a bottle of smoke. You shall lay your plans, and arrange your machinery, and start your schemes; but without the Lord you will do nothing. Immeasurable cloud land of proposals and not a spot of solid doing large enough for a dove's foot to rest on – such shall be the end of all!"

What Spurgeon pointed out was the utter uselessness of doing life apart from the work of Jesus Christ. In these verses, Jesus is front and center as the One in whom we must believe. Faith in Him opens the human heart to a power far greater than anything we could experience in our own strength – we are empowered by the Holy Spirit. He is the key to understanding the life of Christ and living Christ's life fruitfully each day.

The Big Idea

The danger with troubled people is not that they will believe nothing, but that they will believe anything! To avert such loss of truth and certainty in his disciples, Jesus turned their minds to the Father. He offered the personal touch of a heaven where the Father lives, personally prepared by the Son, and containing enough room for all who follow him.

In the Old Testament God spoke of the vine as a symbol of Israel. In John 15 Jesus expanded the analogy. As the fulfillment of the Lord's purpose for Israel, the great son of David identified himself as the vine and his followers as branches. If you look for key words during your Bible study, note the eleven occurrences of "remain" in 15:4-10.

Christ in the Text

In John, Jesus is the Logos, the Word of God who was with God and was God. Jesus is God in flesh. Jesus' deity is further amplified in His seven "I am" sayings "I am the Bread of Life, the light of the world, the door of the sheep, the good Shepherd, the resurrection and the life, the way, the truth, and the life, the true vine."

#1 He Assures You of Heaven (John 14:1-4)

"Let not your hearts be troubled. Believe in God; believe also in me. In my Father's house are many rooms. If it were not so, would I have told you that I go to prepare a place for you? And if I go and prepare a place for you, I will come again and will take you to myself, that where I am you may be also. And you know the way to where I am going."
~ John 14:1-4

1. Why was faith in Christ the way the disciples could find peace for their troubled hearts? What about their journey to this point could give them the peace they needed?

2. What do Jesus' words tell us about Heaven?

2 He is the Only Path to the Father (John 14:5-11)

Thomas said to him, "Lord, we do not know where you are going. How can we know the way?" Jesus said to him, "I am the way, and the truth, and the life. No one comes to the Father except through me. If you had known me, you would have known my Father also. From now on you do know him and have seen him."

Philip said to him, "Lord, show us the Father, and it is enough for us." Jesus said to him, "Have I been with you so long, and you still do not know me, Philip? Whoever has seen me has seen the Father. How can you say, 'Show us the Father'? Do you not believe that I am in the Father and the Father is in me? The words that I say to you I do not speak on my own authority, but the Father who dwells in me does his works. Believe me that I am in the Father and the Father is in me, or else believe on account of the works themselves.
~ John 14:5-11

1. Why is the exclusivity of Christ's claim bothersome to an unbelieving world? Why do you think some Christians struggle with it?

2. Jesus said, "Whoever has seen me has seen the Father." What can you learn about the character and nature of God through the life of Jesus as revealed in the New Testament?

3. How does it practically inform the way you live, lead your family and make decisions?

3 He is the Answer to Your Prayers (John 14:12-14)

"Truly, truly, I say to you, whoever believes in me will also do the works that I do; and greater works than these will he do, because I am going to the Father. Whatever you ask in my name, this I will do, that the Father may be glorified in the Son. If you ask me anything in my name, I will do it.
~ John 14:12-14

1. Jesus said, "Whoever believes in me will also do the works I do; and greater works than these will he do" What does He mean?

2. What does Jesus mean when He says that we can ask anything in His name and He will do it? How might this correspond to the previous verse?

4 He is the One Who Sends You the Holy Spirit (John 14:15-24)

"If you love me, you will keep my commandments. And I will ask the Father, and he will give you another Helper, to be with you forever, even the Spirit of truth, whom the world cannot receive, because it neither sees him nor knows him. You know him, for he dwells with you and will be in you. "I will not leave you as orphans; I will come to you. Yet a little while and the world will see me no more, but you will see me. Because I live, you also will live. In that day you will know that I am in my Father, and you in me, and I in you.

Whoever has my commandments and keeps them, he it is who loves me. And he who loves me will be loved by my Father, and I will love him and manifest myself to him." Judas (not Iscariot) said to him, "Lord, how is it that you will manifest yourself to us, and not to the world?" Jesus answered him, "If anyone loves me, he will keep my word, and my Father will love him, and we will come to him and make our home with him. Whoever does not love me does not keep my words. And the word that you hear is not mine but the Father's who sent me.
~ John 14:15-24

1. According to this passage, what is the work of the Holy Spirit?

2. What are the implications of Jesus' correlation between keeping His commandments and loving Him?

5 He is Your Peace (John 14:25-31)

"These things I have spoken to you while I am still with you. But the Helper, the Holy Spirit, whom the Father will send in my name, he will teach you all things and bring to your remembrance all that I have said to you. Peace I leave with you; my peace I give to you. Not as the world gives do I give to you. Let not your hearts be troubled, neither let them be afraid. You heard me say to you, 'I am going away, and I will come to you.' If you loved me, you would have rejoiced, because I am going to the Father, for the Father is greater than I. And now I have told you before it takes place, so that when it does take place you may believe. I will no longer talk much with you, for the ruler of this world is coming. He has no claim on me, but I do as the Father has commanded me, so that the world may know that I love the Father. Rise, let us go from here."
~ John 14:15-24

1. How does the peace of God influence difficult moments in your life?

2. What did Jesus mean by "the Father is greater than I?"

6 He is the True Vine (John 15:1-8)

"I am the true vine, and my Father is the vinedresser. Every branch in me that does not bear fruit he takes away, and every branch that does bear fruit he prunes, that it may bear more fruit.

Already you are clean because of the word that I have spoken to you. Abide in me, and I in you. As the branch cannot bear fruit by itself, unless it abides in the vine, neither can you, unless you abide in me. I am the vine; you are the branches. Whoever abides in me and I in him, he it is that bears much fruit, for apart from me you can do nothing. If anyone does not abide in me he is thrown away like a branch and withers; and the branches are gathered, thrown into the fire, and burned.

If you abide in me, and my words abide in you, ask whatever you wish, and it will be done for you. By this my Father is glorified, that you bear much fruit and so prove to be my disciples."
~ *John 14:15-24*

1. What is the key to producing the Christian life?

2. How does bearing much fruit glorify the Lord?'

7 He is the One Who Chose You in Love (John 15:9-17)

"I am the true vine, and my Father is the vinedresser. Every branch in me that does not bear fruit he takes away, and every branch that does bear fruit he prunes, that it may bear more fruit. Already you are clean because of the word that I have spoken to you. Abide in me, and I in you.

As the branch cannot bear fruit by itself, unless it abides in the vine, neither can you, unless you abide in me. I am the vine; you are the branches. Whoever abides in me and I in him, he it is that bears much fruit, for apart from me you can do nothing. If anyone does not abide in me he is thrown away like a branch and withers; and the branches are gathered, thrown into the fire, and burned.

If you abide in me, and my words abide in you, ask whatever you wish, and it will be done for you. By this my Father is glorified, that you bear much fruit and so prove to be my disciples."
~ *John 14:15-24*

1. What does it mean to abide in the love of Christ?

2. What kind of love is natural for Christians? How would you describe it? How are you living it out?

3. How does God's choosing you to bear fruit motivate you to live righteously every day?

🦶 Diving Deeper

1. What is the biggest takeaway from this passage?

2. What are some ways you could apply this passage?

3. If Jesus is unique above all others, how will you exhibit this fact to others?

4. What will you apply specifically this week?

"People had only to look at Jesus to see what God is like. People today should only have to look at us to see what Jesus is like."

~ **Randy Alcorn**

GROW Passages for Week 10

1. Matthew 1:18-2:12; Luke 2:1-22; John 1:1-8

2. Matthew 5:1-7:29

3. John 14:1-15:17

4. Matthew 27:1-28:15

5. Matthew 28:16-20; Mark 16:14-18; Luke 24:45-49

SESSION 11

The Great Kick Start

Acts 1-11; 2:1-47

Around 1885, the first motorcycle came on the scene. It was rudimentary, but it began a long history of motorcycle evolution that continues to bring joy to millions who ride each year. In 1919, a new phrase was coined as the internal combustion engine had to be "kickstarted" by the rider placing their foot on the pedal and pushing downward. The word kickstart now serves other purposes such as describing when a new company gets an influx of cash to get off the ground or when taxes are lowered to kickstart the economy. The word can be used to also describe the activity surrounding the launch of the early church.

After Jesus's death and crucifixion, he appeared to his disciples and around 500 people before his ascension into the heavens. He told them to wait in Jerusalem until they were empowered by the Holy Spirit who would make them his witnesses in Jerusalem, Judea, Samaria and the uttermost parts of the world (Acts 1:8). The infusion of power by the Holy Spirit in Acts 2 launched the church with 3,000 souls responding to the first church sermon by Peter.

The kickstart immediately impacted the surrounding cities and countries. People began to live differently. They no longer went to the pagan temples for worship but believed in Jesus Christ alone.

The people sold possessions to help others in need, enemies became friends, kindness became normal, and selflessness became the natural way of living. Sacrifice no longer meant taking animals to the pagan festivals. Marriages were restored, a woman's status within the church equaled that of a man, and children were longer viewed as possessions. No one held on to their property selfishly but willingly gave what others needed.

Slaves fellowshipped with owners as equals, racism was denounced, abuse confronted, and a radical willingness to share the gospel everywhere with everyone became the mission. The Church was born! The world had changed. Nothing would be the same! If you are in Christ, you belong to the long line of believers who impact and influence this world every day. How are you contributing to this mission?

Connecting to the Story

You're in charge of recruiting people to a team you've started. This could be a sports team, a business startup, a barber shop quartet, etc. What would your start-up be and out of everyone in the world, who are your top two picks?

Diving into the Story

What's It All About
Acts 1:1-11 and all of Act 2 combined is not a small portion of scripture. Having 58 verses in total, it's easy to break those up into smaller sections. The "titles" of these sections entice us to separate the narrative into bite size chunks, but this can cause us to sometimes miss the overarching idea. From the moment Jesus ascends into heaven to when the new believers are exploring how to be in community with one another, it's all centered around the birth of the Church.

Christ gave the disciples the command to be His witnesses to the world. God sent them the Holy Spirit as a helper to allow them to do this work well. The Holy Spirit is poured out on the disciples and allowed them to speak in different languages, which in turn gave them a platform to tell the masses about the Gospel.

In the end, more than 3,000 joined their numbers. God's goal the whole time was to prepare his workers for the harvest that was coming and to set them up to lead the churches that would come out of this first encounter. God's plan for spreading the good news and for glorifying God are the people called, "The Church". These passages give us a look into how the Lord did it and how it should be done now.

The Big Idea

We must remember that the Holy Spirit is present in every believer and we must be actively aware of what His role is. The Spirit of God came because God is the fuel for the fire. Everything that takes place in these verses can only happen because of God's power and sovereignty, not any of our own.

Christ in the Text

How can one sum this up succinctly? Jesus and his work and legacy are the basis for this whole text. Christ ascends in the very beginning of Acts and is the start of the catalyst that brings about the Church. Before He goes though, He tells them to wait for the helper to come and fill them with power so they can be his witnesses.

Once the Spirit comes, the first thing that is done with that power is to preach about Jesus to a crowd, and then those who believed and joined the disciples devoted themselves to their teachings about Christ. There was no step of the process that Jesus was not the focal point, the reason why and the way it was accomplished.

#1 Jesus Taken into Heaven (Acts 1:1-11)

"In the first book, O Theophilus, I have dealt with all that Jesus began to do and teach, until the day when he was taken up, after he had given commands through the Holy Spirit to the apostles whom he had chosen. He presented himself alive to them after his suffering by many proofs, appearing to them during forty days and speaking about the kingdom of God.

And while staying with them he ordered them not to depart from Jerusalem, but to wait for the promise of the Father, which, he said, "you heard from me; for John baptized with water, but you will be baptized with the Holy Spirit not many days from now." So when they had come together, they asked him, "Lord, will you at this time restore the kingdom to Israel?" He said to them, "It is not for you to know times or seasons that the Father has fixed by his own authority.

But you will receive power when the Holy Spirit has come upon you, and you will be my witnesses in Jerusalem and in all Judea and Samaria, and to the end of the earth." And when he had said these things, as they were looking on, he was lifted up, and a cloud took him out of their sight. And while they were gazing into heaven as he went, behold, two men stood by them in white robes, and said, "Men of Galilee, why do you stand looking into heaven? This Jesus, who was taken up from you into heaven, will come in the same way as you saw him go into heaven."
~ Acts 1:1-11

1. How does God's perceived temporary absence amplify his presence when the people see him after the resurrection?

2. Knowing that Jesus is resurrected, how does this fact change the way they understand their mission in Acts 1:8?

3. How does Jesus' physical absence enable you to do greater works than Jesus did while on the earth?

2 The Holy Spirit is Poured Out (Acts 2:1-13)

When the day of Pentecost arrived, they were all together in one place. And suddenly there came from heaven a sound like a mighty rushing wind, and it filled the entire house where they were sitting. And divided tongues as of fire appeared to them and rested on each one of them. And they were all filled with the Holy Spirit and began to speak in other tongues as the Spirit gave them utterance. Now there were dwelling in Jerusalem Jews, devout men from every nation under heaven. And at this sound the multitude came together, and they were bewildered, because each one was hearing them speak in his own language. And they were amazed and astonished, saying, "Are not all these who are speaking Galileans? And how is it that we hear, each of us in his own native language? Parthians and Medes and Elamites and residents of Mesopotamia, Judea and Cappadocia, Pontus and Asia, Phrygia and Pamphylia, Egypt and the parts of Libya belonging to Cyrene, and visitors from Rome, both Jews and proselytes, Cretans and Arabians—we hear them telling in our own tongues the mighty works of God." And all were amazed and perplexed, saying to one another, "What does this mean?" But others mocking said, "They are filled with new wine."
~ Acts 2:1-13

1. To what degree do you grasp the magnitude of what it means to have the Holy Spirit living within you?

2. How could living from the fullness of that knowledge affect where you live, work and play?

3 Peter Speaks (Acts 2:14-40)

"Men of Israel, hear these words: Jesus of Nazareth, a man attested to you by God with mighty works and wonders and signs that God did through him in your midst, as you yourselves know—this Jesus, delivered up according to the definite plan and foreknowledge of God, you crucified and killed by the hands of lawless men.

God raised him up, loosing the pangs of death, because it was not possible for him to be held by it."
~ *Acts 2:22-24 (2:14-40)*

1. What has evangelism looked like for you in the past, or how do you picture it looking in your future?

2. If you were talking to someone about who Jesus was, what sources or experiences would you use to back up your claims?

4 The Beginnings of the Church (Acts 2:41-47)

So those who received his word were baptized, and there were added that day about three thousand souls.
And they devoted themselves to the apostles' teaching and the fellowship, to the breaking of bread and the prayers. And awe came upon every soul, and many wonders and signs were being done through the apostles. And all who believed were together and had all things in common. And they were selling their possessions and belongings and distributing the proceeds to all, as any had need. And day by day, attending the temple together and breaking bread in their homes, they received their food with glad and generous hearts, praising God and having favor with all the people. And the Lord added to their number day by day those who were being saved.
~ *Acts 2:41-47*

1. Looking at the church today, where do you see areas where we could take a lesson from the early church in Acts?

2. How could you and your family take steps to be a part of that change?

Diving Deeper

1. What is the biggest takeaway from this passage?

2. If you were going to launch a church, what would it look like?

3. What are some ways you could apply this passage?

4. What will you apply specifically this week?

"It's not so much that the church has a mission, it's that the mission of God has a church.
~ **Alan Hirsch.**"

GROW Passages for Week 11

1. Acts 1:1-11; 2:1-47

2. Acts 4:1-22; 5:1-11; 6:8-8:1

3. Acts 9:1-31

4. Acts 10:1-48

5. Acts 16:1-18:28

The Power of the Gospel

Romans 3:1-31; 5:1-21

Christina was tired of living at home under the rule of her mom. She wanted freedom to make her own choices, go her own way and do whatever she wanted when she wanted. Finally, Christina did it. She left home in search of her own life. The farther she went from home, the lonelier she felt, and soon her money ran out. She had nowhere to go and no real friends, not to mention, she would never be able to go home and face the shame of leaving of family without saying goodbye.

Hungry, desperate, depressed, and broke, Christina turned to prostitution. For weeks, she went from one motel to the next. Everything in her body and soul felt the pain of being used as a commodity. Her dignity was gone, and all she felt was a burning sense of shame, regret and loneliness. She longed for home, but thought home was too far from her mistakes.

From the moment Christina left home, her mom looked desperately from town to town and from city to city. One day she received a tip that Christina was staying in a certain city. Christina's mom went there immediately. She went into a picture booth and produced several small-framed pictures of herself. She placed the small pictures in motels, diners, street corners and anywhere she thought Christina might see.

One morning, Christina walked out of a motel room and went to the phone at the front desk. By the phone she noticed a small picture. To her astonishment, she recognized the person in the frame. Christina's eyes filled with tears as she looked into the face of her mother. She turned the picture over and, on the back, her mom had written, "Dear Christina, No matter what you have done. No matter what you have become. All is forgiven. I love you!"

In that moment, the weight of all her shame and guilt fell. Christina called her mom and she once again found home. That is the power of the gospel. The message of the gospel says we have rebelled against our Creator, rejected His life and turned our back to go our own way. But the gospel also says Christ suffered, died and rose from the dead to provide forgiveness and deliverance from the penalty of our sin. In Romans 3, Paul spells out the reality of humanity's condition and reveals the only remedy for humanity's condition.

Connecting to the Story

How does the truth of Romans chapters three and five help us to answer why the practice of religious rituals to earn God's favor and salvation are both impossible and unnecessary? Why is it important to understand your sinful state to appreciate the good news of salvation?

Diving into the Story

What's It All About
How can a person be saved? That question has been the subject of discussion in church history for two thousand years. Romans 3 through 8 gives the answer most clearly.

Grant Osborne writes, "Those who think we participate in producing our salvation need to listen to the clarion call of the sovereignty of God in salvation. Those who believe we can earn it by our works must listen to the emphasis on the sacrifice of Christ as the only basis for salvation."

"God presented Christ as a sacrifice of atonement, through the shedding of his blood—to be received by faith. He did this to demonstrate his righteousness, because in his forbearance he had left the sins committed beforehand unpunished—he did it to demonstrate his righteousness at the present time, so as to be just and the one who justifies those who have faith in Jesus." (3:25-26) Are you afraid to die?

Paul will outline the Good News of Jesus Christ in chapters 3 and 5 that will bring conviction yet lead to the assurance of hope we have in our redemption and salvation through Jesus. God is a holy God and cannot allow sinners into heaven. As God is holy, He is also love and has made a way for sinners to be redeemed. "For everyone has sinned" (Rom. 3:23) ...yet God, in His grace, freely makes us right in His sight. He did this through Christ Jesus when he freed us from the penalty for our sins.

Why did God take our place and bear our sin? John Stott writes, "it would be hard to exaggerate the magnitude of the changes which have taken place as a result of the cross, both in God and in us, especially in God's dealings with us and in our relations with him. Truly, when Christ died and was raised from death, a new day dawned, a new age began."

"For he says, "In the time of my favor I heard you, and in the day of salvation I helped you." I tell you, now is the time of God's favor, now is the day of salvation." (2Cor 6:2) The salvation of Christ is illustrated by the vivid imagery of terms like propitiation, redemption, justification and reconciliation.

The book of Romans introduces us to several images of salvation through propitiation, redemption, justification and reconciliation. Images instead of theories is a better term according to John Stott. "For theories are usually abstract and speculative concepts, whereas the biblical images of the atoning achievement of Christ are concrete pictures and belong to the data of revelation.

They are not alternative explanations of the cross, providing us with a range to choose from, but complementary to one another, each contributing a vital part to the whole. As for the imagery, propitiation introduces us to rituals at a shrine, redemption to transactions in a market-place, justification to proceedings in a lawcourt, and reconciliation to experiences in a home or family."

The Big Idea

Sin has completely broken our relationship with God. "For all have sinned and fall short of the glory of God." However, God made a way to restore that relationship through Jesus Christ. "Therefore, since we have been justified through faith, we have peace with God through our Lord Jesus Christ."

Christ in the Text

Where is Christ not in the text? Paul takes chapters 3 and 5 to develop the complete story of salvation through Jesus. What we could not do by ourselves, Christ has already done for us. Jesus took our punishment on the cross, died in our place and shed his blood for us. "So just as sin ruled over all people and brought them to death, now God's wonderful grace rules instead, giving us right standing with God and resulting in eternal life through Jesus Christ our Lord." John Stott sums it up well, "If God in Christ did not die in our place, there could be neither propitiation, nor redemption, nor justification, nor reconciliation."

#1 God Remains Faithful (Romans 3:1-8)

Then what advantage has the Jew? Or what is the value of circumcision? Much in every way. To begin with, the Jews were entrusted with the oracles of God. What if some were unfaithful? Does their faithlessness nullify the faithfulness of God? By no means! Let God be true though everyone were a liar, as it is written, "That you may be justified in your words, and prevail when you are judged." But if our unrighteousness serves to show the righteousness of God, what shall we say? That God is unrighteous to inflict wrath on us? (I speak in a human way.) By no means! For then how could God judge the world? But if through my lie God's truth abounds to his glory, why am I still being condemned as a sinner? And why not do evil that good may come?—as some people slanderously charge us with saying. Their condemnation is just.
~ Romans 3:1-8

1. What does it mean that the Jews were entrusted with the gospel? How did this hold them accountable to God's message to the world?

2. Why did Paul say that Israel's faithlessness did not nullify the faithfulness of God? What does that say about the nature of God and its impact on your life?

2 All People are Sinners (Romans 3:9-20)

"Now we know that whatever the law says it speaks to those who are under the law, so that every mouth may be stopped, and the whole world may be held accountable to God. For by works of the law no human being will be justified in his sight, since through the law comes knowledge of sin."
~ Romans 3:19-20 (3:9-20)

1. Are these verses offensive in this culture? Why?

2. Are they offensive to you? If so, why? If not, why?

3. What are the implications of being accountable to God?

3 Christ Took our Punishment (Romans 3:21-31)

"But now the righteousness of God has been manifested apart from the law, although the Law and the Prophets bear witness to it the righteousness of God through faith in Jesus Christ for all who believe. For there is no distinction: for all have sinned and fall short of the glory of God, and are justified by his grace as a gift, through the redemption that is in Christ Jesus, whom God put forward as a propitiation by his blood, to be received by faith. This was to show God's righteousness, because in his divine forbearance he had passed over former sins. It was to show his righteousness at the present time, so that he might be just and the justifier of the one who has faith in Jesus."
~ Romans 3:21-26 (3:21-31)

1. Why is no one innocent before God?

2. How does Paul describe the manner in which Christ became our substitute?

3. In what do you have to boast if Christ is the justifier of the one who has faith in Jesus Christ?

4 Faith Brings Joy (Romans 5:1-11)

Therefore, since we have been justified by faith, we have peace with God through our Lord Jesus Christ. Through him we have also obtained access by faith into this grace in which we stand, and we rejoice in hope of the glory of God.

Not only that, but we rejoice in our sufferings, knowing that suffering produces endurance, and endurance produces character, and character produces hope, and hope does not put us to shame, because God's love has been poured into our hearts through the Holy Spirit who has been given to us. For while we were still weak, at the right time Christ died for the ungodly. For one will scarcely die for a righteous person— though perhaps for a good person one would dare even to die— but God shows his love for us in that while we were still sinners, Christ died for us.

Since, therefore, we have now been justified by his blood, much more shall we be saved by him from the wrath of God. For if while we were enemies we were reconciled to God by the death of his Son, much more, now that we are reconciled, shall we be saved by his life. More than that, we also rejoice in God through our Lord Jesus Christ, through whom we have now received reconciliation.

~ Romans 5:1-11

1. Why is your faith in Christ linked to suffering? Is suffering something you expected when you believed in Christ?

2. How is suffering used in the Christian experience?

5 Adam and Christ Contrasted (Romans 5:12-21)

But the free gift is not like the trespass. For if many died through one man's trespass, much more have the grace of God and the free gift by the grace of that one-man Jesus Christ abounded for many.

And the free gift is not like the result of that one man's sin. For the judgment following one trespass brought condemnation, but the free gift following many trespasses brought justification. For if, because of one man's trespass, death reigned through that one man, much more will those who receive the abundance of grace and the free gift of righteousness reign in life through the one-man Jesus Christ.
~ Romans 5:15-17 (5:12-21)

1. How could this paragraph be the core of Paul's letter?

2. How does Christ change the paradigm of humanity in light of Adam's sin?

👣 Diving Deeper

1. What is the biggest takeaway from this passage?

2. If you were going to launch a church, what would it look like?

3. What are some ways you could apply this passage?

4. What will you apply specifically this week?

"The gospel is not a message about we need to do for God, but about what God has done for us."
~ Kevin DeYoung

GROW Passages for Week 12

1. Acts 1:1-11; 2:1-47

2. Acts 4:1-22; 5:1-11; 6:8-8:1

3. Acts 9:1-31

4. Acts 10:1-48

5. Acts 16:1-18:28

References

Alexander, Desmond. *Obadiah, Jonah, Micah: An Introduction & Commentary*. D.J. Wiseman, General Editor. Leicester: Intervarsity Press, 1988.

Boice, James M. *The Gospel of John: Volume 4 Peace in the Storm, John 13-17*. Grand Rapids: Baker Books, 1985.

Collins, Jim. *Good to Great*. New York: Harper Business Publishers, 2001.

Evans, Tony. *Tony Evans' Book of Illustrations: Stories, Quotes and Anecdotes*. Chicago: Moody Publishers, 2009.

Hannah, John D. *Exodus: The Bible Knowledge Commentary*. Wheaton: Essee Publications, 1985.

Harrison, R.K. *Exodus: The Wycliffe Exegetical Commentary*. Chicago: Moody Press, 1990.

HCSB Study Bible. Nashville: Holman Bible Publishers, 2010.

Katongale, Emmanuel and Chris Rice. *Reconciling All Things: A Christian Vision for Justice, Peace and Healing*. Downers Grover: Intervarsity Press, 2008.

Lucado, Max. *Six hours One Friday*. Nashville: Thomas Nelson, 1988.

Rawlinson, George. *Exodus: The Pulpit Commentary, Volume 1*. Peabody: Hendrickson Publishers, 2000.

Spurgeon, Charles. *The Treasure of David: Volume 1 Psalms 1-87*. Nashville: Thomas Nelson, 1984.

Stott, John R.W. *The Radical Disciple: Some Neglected Aspects of Our Calling*. Downer's Grove: Intervarsity Press, 2010.

Made in the USA
Columbia, SC
15 July 2024

38390289R00061